Aging Adventurously at 80

How I Wrote a Book & Got It Published

SANDRA RICHMOND

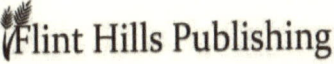

Flint Hills Publishing

Cover Design by Amy Albright
stonypointgraphics.weebly.com

Author Photo by Jonathan Richmond

⫯Flint Hills Publishing

Topeka, Kansas
Tucson, Arizona

www.flinthillspublishing.com

Printed in the U.S.A.

Paperback Book: ISBN 978-1-966323-31-0
Electronic Book ISBN 978-1-966323-33-4

Dedication

To Rachel and Jonathan.
You fill my life with love.
Because of you, I am whole.

Contents

Contents Continued...

Introduction

Have you ever dreamed of writing a book? Did you nod yes? We have something in common!

My dream started more than 25 years ago, but I don't think I realized how many people had the same dream until 2024, my big year, the year I turned 80 and my first book, *Milepost 75: Aging and Exploring Life Trails with Wonder, Resilience, and Love* was published.

I had originally thought selling 1,000 copies would be a reasonable and rational goal. I quickly learned the world was not anxiously waiting to read a story about an unknown, aging woman who changed her life by hiking the Grand Canyon.

But even sans big book sales, I received many other benefits.

One benefit was that a weight had been lifted. That unfulfilled dream of writing my book was finally achieved. I no longer felt like I was carrying around that heavy *did not finish* in my head.

Another benefit was my brain felt stronger. During my career as an operations manager at the telephone company, I loved being able to create. I designed reports that depicted results in a way that motivated my team, showing them how they were making progress. Later at Walt Disney World and Limited Brands where I worked in organization and leadership development, I conducted organization assessments that provided insights with interview summaries that helped to inform and influence my team's behavior. It was fun to see their *ahah* reaction as they learned something new about themselves, their organization, how they could work together, improve, and get stronger. Now readers were telling me I had written a story that delighted them, informed, excited, and even inspired them to change their behavior. I was creating again in a way that could make a difference. It was gratifying to exercise my influence muscles again.

My memoir also created stronger connections with others: family, friends, even strangers via a link of shared memories and experiences.

And maybe the biggest benefit of all was I learned so much about myself. Isn't that interesting? I wrote. Then I read what I wrote and learned things that had never dawned on me before. Lessons from each event, trip, and adventure. Lessons from failure, picking myself up, and trying again. Lessons from the way my late husband, Arnie, and I created a mutually satisfying and rewarding retirement.

I embraced more reasons to be grateful. I discovered a new life purpose. My life has been changed for good. Because I wrote my book.

While many readers have told me they enjoyed reading about my events and adventures and were even inspired by my life story, they were equally if not more intrigued with how I managed to capture my big dream of writing my book and getting it published. Especially after it sat in my head for more than 25 years. Especially at this advanced age.

"Thank you for sending me your book!" my neurosurgeon said as he walked into the exam room for my post-fusion-surgery check-in.

"You're welcome!" I paused, smiled, "Did you read it yet?"

"Well, I read *my* chapter," he said with a big grin. We both laughed.

"And I'm looking forward to reading the rest on the plane on my honeymoon trip."

"I hope you enjoy it. Most people say they loved reading my book, but what they really want to know is how I managed to write a book and get it published."

His face lit up. "That's exactly what I want to know! I want to do that too." And that's it. After folks tell me they enjoyed reading my book (or, even just a chapter), quite often their next question is, "So, how did you manage to write a book and get it published at 80?" They continue with something along the lines of, "I have a book in my head too. I want to write a book like you. I have this story, but I can't get started. How did you do it? Get unstuck? Stick with it? Finish it? And get it published?"

I give short answers. I give long answers. Most ask for even more detail. They stand, stare, and wait for more specifics. They tell me about the spectacular stories in their heads. They want to get unstuck. They want to know how I finally did it.

I listened to my readers and began to wonder if I could write a book that could answer their questions. I decided I could and started writing.

As I wrote, it occurred to me that maybe this book might even inspire them to write that book lodged in their head. After all, I had just finished writing a book that inspired readers to get unstuck and get out to walk. It wasn't a how-to-get-fit book. It was a story of how I embraced an active life in my mid-forties.

So that's what I did. This is that book.

But here is my caveat: This is not a *how-to* book. It is not a book on how to become a best-selling author. It's a book about how I achieved my goal. My journey. My results. My way.

My experiences are unique. The steps I took. The paths I navigated through grief and gratitude. The hills and valleys I traversed. The lessons I learned. I was fortunate in terms of timing and resources with no imposed deadlines or need to make a living through my writing. My life was full. I was living the dream I had yearned for when I was younger. I was comfortably retired in my 70s with control over how I invested my time.

As I wrote, other questions guided personal reflection on my writing process. "How did you get started, especially after all those years?" "How did you deal with writer's block?" These questions and many others helped me to dig even deeper, reflect on the many aspects of my writing odyssey and even answer a few questions of my own. They created a new awareness of the opportunities, situations, decisions, even struggles that had an impact on my writing process.

And so, I decided to write a book that answered questions *and* shared my lessons learned. If you are curious. If you want to write that book snuggled in your head. Let's sit down with a cup of coffee or tea and I will share my story with you.

Since this book is another memoir, I doubt you can use it as your roadmap. But maybe it will answer some of your questions. And perhaps you can enjoy being an armchair traveler with me on my writing journey, glean a few ideas and approaches, and maybe even be inspired.

I hope you enjoy tagging along on my book-writing adventure from early inspiration to final accomplishment. Another dream captured. Another reason to be grateful.

So, let's get started!

Background

If you read *Milepost 75*, you know my story began in an article-writing class in Tucson, Arizona more than 30 years ago. One of our assignments was to ask a question that could end up being the source of an article. My question was, "Do any of you know of a way to hike across the Grand Canyon from the South Rim to the North Rim without backpacking, in a short period of time, and very cheap?" After I answered a few questions regarding my outlandish question, one woman provided an answer. She told me about a Grand Canyon 50/24 hike that involved hiking from the South Rim to the North Rim, and then back to the South Rim, a rim-to-rim-to-rim, with an extra side-trail included to make it 50 miles along with the additional requirement to complete it in 24 hours to earn the right to purchase the commemorative T-shirt.

I ended up doing just that. Eventually.

My daughter, Rachel, and I attempted it twice. I tried a third time alone. During this three-year quest, I broke my foot, was plagued with blisters and bad-fitting shoes, even briefly started to doubt myself, but I preservered until that momentous day when I hiked into the abyss around 4:00 a.m. in May 1994 on my fourth attempt. This was the day I finally completed the entire 50-mile hike within the 24-hour time limit, the year I turned 50.

I had earned the right to buy the shirt!

I still have it.

This experience created a seismic shift in me. I developed a new and compelling passion. A fierce drive that sometimes I didn't understand. My fitness priorities were adjusted. As each year passed, my life became more active and more adventurous. I refused to give up when I got waylaid. I didn't let fear of failure stop me from attempting something new. After completing that rim-to-rim-to-rim 50/24, my altered life story was too big to ignore. I wanted to write a book. And many years later, that's exactly what I did.

I'm still reeling from all the excitement of 2024 with turning 80 in February and my first book being published in March. Now, in addition to my other proud roles of mother, grandma, mother-in-law, aunt, cousin, friend, neighbor, volunteer, I can add the title of author! I'm navigating a whole new world, experiencing, learning, entering a new community of colleagues and friends.

I'm also a widow. It's a role I struggle to accept. My husband, Arnie, died almost three years ago. I'm still healing. I still feel a pang when I check "widow" on my appointment forms. I used to be so proud to check "married," especially after we celebrated our golden anniversary.

I'm also grateful for our many years together. We were fortunate, had a good life, were married almost 54 years, raised two wonderful children, Rachel and Jonathan, and have four awesome grandsons.

I live alone in Florida around eight months a year, close to my son, Jonathan and daughter-in-law, Lauren (Jonathan and Lauren are divorced, but we are still family), and grandsons Flip (also a "Jonathan") and Samuel.

And I live in Maryland with daughter, Rachel, son-in-law, Rob, and grandson, Andrew for two months every spring and two months every fall. Their oldest son and my oldest grandson, another Jonathan, serves in the U.S. Army and is currently stationed in Alaska.

Among other things, like enjoying family time, participating in book talks for *Milepost 75,* training for another Grand Canyon hike, and other adventures, I'm journaling and jotting notes for a third book tentatively titled *Milepost 81.*

And I just finished writing my second book, this book, that

answers all those questions folks have been asking since *Milepost 75* was published and also shares my many lessons learned.

So, here it goes.

PART I

My Path to Writing

HOW DID YOU FINALLY GET UNSTUCK AND START WRITING YOUR BOOK?

Getting unstuck started with an adventure. 2018 was a big year for me and Arnie. Our 50th anniversary was coming up in December. We did not want a big party. Not our style. Didn't want the kids to spend time, money, and effort on festivities. Did not want to take a long trip together. We wanted to celebrate our golden anniversary all year long with a focus on health and wellness, short trips, and family visits.

For our big splurge, we decided to spend two weeks at a health spa on Hilton Head Island in July. Although the drive from our home in Palm Coast, Florida was less than 250 miles, around four hours driving time, we managed to turn that journey into a multi-day adventure. It's what we tended to do. We spent the first night with our son, Jonathan, and two grandsons, Flip and Sam, in his home at Fernandina Beach. Then we stayed two nights in Savanna, Georgia where we saw our first container boat as we strolled along River Street. We stopped in our tracks. Amazed! We were easily impressed. We also drove out to tour Fort Pulaski National Monument after seeing the sign on Highway 95 for way too many years. I *love* visiting national parks and monuments! My National Park Passport Book is filled with stamps and stickers. Such a delightful quest.

We finally checked into the health spa on Sunday afternoon, already congratulating ourselves on our 50th anniversary celebration strategy.

On Wednesday, Arnie and I walked into the dining room for another healthy, tasty breakfast. We noticed a woman, someone we hadn't seen before, sitting alone at a small table. Of course, Arnie waved and said, "Hi. Do you want to join us?"

She looked up, cocked her head, smiled, hesitated just a moment, then gathered up her stuff and came over to our table.

"Hi. I'm Lynya. I just came in last night and I'm already enjoying myself."

I looked up from my menu (that listed calories instead of prices) and said, "Nice to meet you. I didn't realize you could start in the middle of the week. We're staying for two weeks. How long will you be here? Oops—sorry, I'm Sandi."

"And I'm Arnie."

"Nice to meet you!" She looked from side to side, leaned in, and in a soft voice said, "Please keep this to yourselves, but I'm the health editor of *Family Circle* and I'm here to write an article."

Arnie grinned. "Our lips are sealed, but how cool. I can see how spending some time here would make a great story."

I sat back, staring, processing what I had just heard. *I just met the editor for a national magazine! She is an author! She is a celebrity!* I was star struck. I sucked in my breath and wiggled in my chair. I did not want her autograph. I wanted her advice. Could I build up the nerve to ask her?

Lynya continued to join us and others for meals together. She and I got to know each other a little more on several kayaking, hiking, and exploring excursions. She threw herself into every activity. Her enthusiasm was palpable. I imagined the engaging story she would write for *Family Circle*. I watched her in awe, studied her intently, this real, live author.

I really wanted to pick her brain. Ask her a few writing questions, especially about how to get unstuck, but I didn't want to blow her cover or make her feel uncomfortable in any way. It would feel like walking up to a celebrity and asking for an autograph while she was dining with her family. It felt intrusive. A bit risky.

And then, it was Sunday. Time was running out. We sat together at breakfast. "Well, I'm all packed up and ready to go. I'll be heading back to New York after breakfast," Lynya said.

This is my last chance. I was nervous. *I have to do this. What's the worst that can happen?* I took the plunge and jumped in during a brief lull as we lingered over coffee. "Lynya, I don't want to take too much of your time, but I have a writing question. May I have a few minutes with you before you head out?"

Lynya's head shot up. "Sure!" She flashed her big grin. "Let's go out into the hall and sit down."

We walked around the corner into the hallway that was bathed in sunlight. I found a bench by a window filled with leafy, green plants on the outside trying to push their way inside. We sat down. Turned our knees toward each other. "So, what's going on? What do you want to know?" Lynya asked.

"I had a life-changing experience almost 30 years ago, and I've wanted to write a book about it ever since."

Lynya lowered her chin, leaned in, and looked straight at me. "So, what's stopping you? Why aren't you writing?"

Good question! I sat back, took a big breath, and reflected on the writing block that had kept stopping me in my tracks. "Every time I sit down to write, I think of one more journal I should review. I get stalled looking for that journal or another piece of information. I recognize I'm struggling with the same analysis paralysis I dealt with when I was working on my PhD dissertation. Back then, I kept going back to the library for more research instead of writing everything I already knew. It got so bad my advisor banned me from the library," I said shaking my head.

"I'm going to tell you the same thing your advisor told you, Sandi. Forget the journals. Don't even look at them. Just start writing what's in your head. The memories and insights you have now after all these years are what's important. Eventually, you may want to take a look at some of those journals to do a little fact checking, but for now, just sit and write." She stopped. Leaned in a little further. "Write. Start with 15 minutes a day, then 30, then keep increasing. Get all this stuff out of your head. Don't judge or edit. Just write."

I took a big breath, nodded, trying to process this simple solution. *Could it possibly be this easy?* "Thank you!"

She sat back and smiled, "I have lots of resources and references I can send you when I get home. Just email me. And in the meantime, write."

And that's what I did.

Arnie and I returned home. I cleaned off my desk. Set up an inviting and comfortable writing space. Found a safe spot for my coffee cup. Began to write my book. I followed Lynya's guidance and started writing 15 minutes a day. At first it was hard to just keep writing with no researching or editing. It felt sloppy like it was just a bunch of sentences dribbling out of my head. No stories or style, just words. When I finished my 15 minutes, I looked back on what I had written, trying hard not to judge. For a while the 15 minutes felt like forever, but then time started to pass more quickly. I would look up, surprised to see that I had been writing for 30 minutes, then 45, eventually an hour.

In a way, getting started writing my book was like starting to walk longer distances again after each of my joint-replacement surgeries. At first my steps were awkward, uncomfortable. It took forever even to get to the mailbox.

But with my post-surgery walking and now with my writing, I persevered and kept moving forward.

If I felt tempted to stop and look for something in my stack of journals, I resisted the urge, grabbed a Post-it, jotted a short note to myself, stuck it on the edge of my computer screen, and kept writing.

It was still hard not to judge or edit. Sometimes, it was impossible for me to ignore all those squiggly red lines highlighting my errors. When the compulsion was too strong, I took the time to correct my typos, but to my credit, did not stop to correct those red squiggly lines until I had finished writing for the day.

Most of the time I also treated myself to documenting my word and page count at the end of each writing session in a little log. I was making progress! Eventually, I was easily writing at least an hour every day. Moving forward. Step by step.

I emailed Lynya requesting more resources as she had asked me to do. Then I waited. One week. I refreshed my mailbox. Two weeks. Refreshed it again. Nothing. *She's an author. She's an editor. Maybe she's too busy writing her article. Maybe she decided to skip it and skip me. But maybe my email got lost or she just didn't see it. Should I pester her with another email? Yes, I should.*

Lynya had helped me get started writing each day which was a gigantic first step, but I was meandering. There was no structure to my story. Just a series of memories that kept popping up in my mind. I was finally capturing those memories, but I still felt lost.

I *needed* those resources she had offered.

I sucked it up and emailed again, "Hi, Lynya. I sent an email a few weeks ago and I'm thinking it might have gotten lost in transition. I'm following your guidance and writing every day, so thank you for that unlock! You mentioned you could send me a few other references and resources. I'm sure you're swamped but whenever you have time, I'd be delighted to read anything you can send."

Her reply zipped back. "Oh Sandi! I'm so sorry. I had so many emails when I returned, I must have missed your first email. Here are a few articles. Why don't we schedule a call so we can chat and figure out what else you need and how I can help you keep moving forward with your book?"

Thank goodness I did not give up! This was such a good lesson. I needed to remember this. I cannot give up even if I'm embarrassed or insecure. I have so many questions. I have to keep seeking answers and assistance or I will *never* write my book.

Lynya sent several articles. I read them. Then, I checked her website and discovered she was also a writing coach. How fortuitous! When we talked on the phone, I asked if I could hire her.

"Sandi, I'm happy to help you get started. You have a

compelling story, and I believe it would make a great memoir. You don't have to hire me."

"Lynya, I have no formal writing training. I have no idea how to write a book. I know myself well enough that I would not learn enough by taking a class. I can't do this alone. I need help. It would be an honor if you would teach me. Working with you as my writing coach would be another adventure. It would help me capture another big dream. It would be a worthy investment for me if you are willing to take me on."

Lynya laughed, "Okay, let's do it!" We made payment arrangements and set up a meeting schedule.

And that's how my writing journey began. She taught me a process. Then we worked that process. We would email back and forth with quick questions and answers and have deeper discussions on my progress and roadblocks during 50-minute calls every six weeks or so depending on our travel schedules.

Sometimes we would put our work on hold. Family priorities always took precedence. She took care of her parents. Changed jobs. Traveled. Arnie and I traveled too. When Hurricane Dorian slammed Palm Coast in 2019, we evacuated to Georgia for a week. Writing paused as we took day trips exploring national parks. Three more stamps in my little National Park Passport book! Ocmulgee National Monument, Andersonville National Historic Site, and Jimmy Carter National Historic Park. We turned our evacuation into another adventure.

As soon as we returned home, I started writing again, at least an hour a day, but usually longer. My writing began to mimic my walking. The more I wrote, the easier it became, the longer I wrote.

Lynya and I worked together on and off from fall of 2018 to fall of 2022. By then, I had my manuscript ready to submit to a publisher.

When I reflect on my fortuitous meeting with Lynya, I am reminded once more that our lives are filled with opportunities.

We must simply recognize and embrace them. What if Arnie had not asked Lynya to join us? If I hadn't asked to talk to her? If I hadn't followed up when she didn't respond to my first email? Where would I be in my book-writing quest?

I don't believe things are "meant to be." I do believe in seeing and seizing opportunities, taking risks, moving out of my comfort zone, and asking for help. I was lucky. I was fortunate. I had taken the first big step on my book-writing journey. I finally got unstuck. I continue to be grateful to this day.

 WHAT WAS YOUR PURPOSE?

When Lynya first asked me to dig deep and think about my purpose, I struggled. To report? To brag? To record my story for my family? To inspire? Why did I want to write this book? Why was this desire to tell my tale so firmly embedded in my head, heart, and soul? I had always believed my late start in an active lifestyle that began with the Grand Canyon rim-to-rim-to rim 50/24 would make a great story. But would it? Would people want to read it? I didn't break any records. Was this really that big of a deal? I was plagued with doubt. I finally had the assistance and opportunity to write my book; why was I stuck on clarifying my purpose?

Clearly, I needed more time and a few walks to figure this out. I took that time, went on more walks until I could finally shake off all (or at least, most) of my misgivings. Then I articulated my purpose and defined the focus of my memoir. And the best gift of all was that I gave myself permission to adjust my purpose as I moved forward in my writing journey.

At this point, I just needed a place to start.

I walked. I thought. *I am quite ordinary. I want to make my story accessible and interesting. And, since I have done a few amazing things, I want it to be a bit unbelievable. But mostly, I want it to delight and inspire the people who read my story. I want readers to feel encouraged. To feel energized, not overwhelmed.*

I started to feel encouraged. *Maybe my book can make a difference to some readers. Maybe it can even make a difference the way my Grand Canyon 50/24 quest made a difference in my life.* That seemed like a lofty purpose, but I planted that seed anyway. And, as that seed germinated, I kept trying to figure out how I could begin my story.

As both Arnie and I aged, we spent more time visiting doctors. Scans. Blood tests. Physical therapy. I went to my appointments—and Arnie's. And I never considered the time spent on our health care a *demand.* They were opportunities to stay healthy. We were well taken care of with solid insurance and access to practitioners of our choice. We were fortunate with many reasons to be grateful. It was a good and healthy use of our time.

I believed my aging life was very relatable, especially to those who were dealing with their own physical issues. I hoped my book would encourage many readers, to let them know they are not alone. And so, I decided to begin the introduction to *Milepost 75* with a medical story.

A recent doctor's visit had created a sense of urgency with the possibility that I might have to start slowing down. That I may not be able to continue my active lifestyle that had begun all those years ago in the Grand Canyon. She told me to stop walking so much and start focusing more on exercising, biking, and swimming. That was certainly sound medical advice, but, if I couldn't walk as much, I couldn't train for my upcoming adventures.

I was determined to keep moving forward with my plans. I was scared. I was motivated. Even inspired. The core of my book could focus on all the events and adventures I wanted to accomplish in 2019, the year I would turn 75, especially since there was the chance it might be my final year of accomplishing my "impossible" dreams. My spirit was ready to keep going. My body might not be able to comply.

Maybe my story could inspire others to get out and move before it's too late, even if a few things are breaking down. I also thought readers would enjoy reading about some of my 75th year travel adventures.

As soon as I started writing, my purpose shifted and expanded. Looking back at my writing journey, I realize that many chapters of *Milepost 75* were written in response to questions I received from early readers. I wrote chapters to answer questions about how my life was transformed by my Grand Canyon quest in my mid-forties. Readers wanted to know more about how I managed to get a late start in many other aspects of my life and still accomplish so many dreams. How, when I did not score high enough on my first GMAT to be admitted to the PhD program at 46, I simply took classes, studied harder, got a higher score, and entered my PhD program at age 47. How I started participating in marathons and other walker-friendly events at age 55. How I reconnected with my brother, through walking, of course. How I kept moving forward after my surgeries and injuries. How I embraced adventure travel in my 70s after I retired.

I wrote. I shared. I received feedback. I revised. I added. I deleted. My book became more readable. My writing improved.

When I reached the end of my manuscript, it occurred to me that I had written three books merged into one.

Book One was about my 75th birthday year, fearing it might be my last big hurrah, celebrating all year long, and inviting readers to go along for the ride with me.

Book Two included stories about getting a late start, getting older, dealing with emerging body issues, injuries, surgeries, but still moving forward, never giving up. During the years I worked on my book, I got older. I slowed down. I wrote more about needing to walk every day and enjoying it. Although I enjoyed sharing stories of my big adventures, I wanted even more to inspire my readers to make small active differences, to get up, get out, and walk, or at least be outside, moving, every day.

Book Three was about family. Arnie's love, support, and encouragement. My walking relationships with every member of my family, especially Rachel and Jonathan. My long and short walks and big and little trips with children, in-laws, and grandchildren. Savoring precious moments, treating each connection as a gift, never taking anything for granted.

I never imagined what would happen to my life because I wrote *Milepost 75*.

Writing changed me. It informed me. Writing my memoir helped me better understand the unifying themes not only of my book, but also of my life. For example, as I wrote my story, read, and reread, it dawned on me that our habit of taking family walks started way back when Rachel and Jonathan were little. I hadn't remembered that. And, when they grew up, whenever we took those quick, weekend trips to visit our kids and their families while I was still working, we also took family walks. Walking had become a part of our kids' lives too. What a gift that I was able resurrect that sweet memory of our family's walking history.

Writing my book helped me appreciate even more the power of family, how very fortunate I was and still am today. Now that alone was a worthy purpose!

 WHAT WAS YOUR WRITING PROCESS?

Lynya's first assignment was to create an outline. My first outline was simply twelve sections, one for each month of the year 2019, the year I turned 75.

"That's way too predictable, even boring. Nope. Not compelling at all. Try again," said Lynya.

I moved away from a calendar, and imagined a storyline that

would encourage readers to read my memoir with wonder and curiosity, even anticipation. After a series of back and forths, we settled on an outline of 12-14 sections that focused on events, challenges, and adventures, with a sense of urgency and even a hint of suspense.

I knew the outline would still need to be adjusted, but my manuscript was beginning to take shape.

Her next assignment was to write a purpose statement for each section of the outline. This was a huge breakthrough! In fact, as I think back, clarifying my purpose for each section was probably one of the most precious insights Lynya gave me.

For each section I asked myself, what was my purpose? What did I want to convey? Why would this section be interesting to my readers? How would it move my story forward? What was my roadmap? My direction? My boundaries? What did I want to include—and not include? How could I tie everything together? I pondered each section and created a purpose statement. Sometimes, as I expanded each section, I would adjust my purpose.

But now I had a framework. An approach. A process.

On my own, I decided to include at least one lesson in almost every section. My purpose statement at the beginning and key lesson at the end served as bookends for almost every section.

Then, Lynya gave me the next big step.

She told me to take each section with its purpose statement and write a story. Just one story.

As I wrote each story, new stories emerged. For example, I wrote a story about my ballet exercise class, then decided to include a story about my Tai Chi class too. This allowed me to share a precious conversation with my Tai Chi peer who had recently been diagnosed with Alzheimer's.

I gave myself permission to add stories and expand existing ones. Even if we ended up deleting some later, I was determined to empty my brain. This was not the time to hold back.

In another section I wrote a paragraph for each of my trips to China, Spain, Israel, and Peru. In each paragraph, I included several highlights of each trip. When Lynya read this section, she said my writing was getting *listy*. "Go back to each place, picture yourself there, remember those moments that would help your reader join you on your journey."

The lists turned into stories. The stories expanded, became richer with detail. The paragraphs became pages.

These expanded and more detailed stories ended up providing the opportunity for readers to become armchair travelers, exploring far-away locales, sharing my challenges and joy, learning new lessons.

The sections grew. They turned into chapters. I kept referring to my chapter bookends of purpose and lesson to help guide my story telling. How did my stories relate to my purpose? What lessons did I want to share? In some cases, I adjusted my purpose and added different lessons. In most cases they served as gentle guideposts, keeping me focused and on track.

I kept writing. I rearranged and renamed chapters. Merged a few. Separated others. Deleted some and incorporated key points into other chapters. My final version included 16 chapters with an Introduction and an Afterward. My memoir was taking shape and moving forward with flow.

I gave each chapter my best shot and then sent it to Lynya. The chapters were not always in order. Some chapters were easier to write than others. In fact, I saved the first two chapters about the rim-to-rim-to-rim journey and our final years in Tucson until the last. They were such a big part of my story. They were so big I struggled to condense those years into just a few chapters. Even though I wanted to clear out my head, I couldn't write everything. Those first two chapters could have easily ended up being a book. But that wasn't my goal. The point of my memoir was that these events had changed my life. So, I whittled and fine-tuned, trying to figure out the most important segments. In some cases, I cut out too much. Later, my editor, Paul, helped me add depth of feeling and subtract dry reporting of facts.

 ## DID YOU GET STRESSED WHEN YOU WROTE?

Occasionally, yes. Most of the time I wrote with joy. It was relaxing, exhilarating, and fun. But, although I was rarely at a loss for words, there were times when I would get stressed and stalled. The words were still in my head waiting to be written, but they would get smothered by a blanket of worry. I would start thinking about the future. I'd get sad wondering if anyone would ever want to read my book. I'd feel overwhelmed with doubt. Would my memoir ever be good enough?

When I got bogged down and plagued with fear, I'd take a break, take a walk, and even make up walking-writing mantras like this:

Slow, stall, sad.

Words, worry, wisdom.

Perspective, present, peace.

This little ditty would keep me going for at least a few hundred steps, make me smile, give me energy, help me pick up my pace—both walking and writing.

Even as the words continued to flow, I'd continue to worry about the future. *What if I can't find a publisher? What if I have to self-publish? I don't know how to self-publish. This is all so scary!*

I shared my fears with Lynya. She shared her perspective. Her most frequent coaching during those down times was, "Remember your joy! Recapture that feeling you always rely on during your adventures. You walk, you climb, and you hike with passion and satisfaction, in the moment, savoring every step. Now do the same with your writing. Just keep moving forward. Enjoy your journey." Lynya's wisdom kept me going. I would return to writing with joy.

At least for a while.

When I needed another lift, she provided her most powerful insight. "Just focus on the present. Look at how far you have come. You love to write. Your words are flowing. You frequently write hours a day. Stop thinking and obsessing about the future. *Be here now* with your computer. Sit and write."

Lynya helped me navigate the emotional side of writing along with the actual, physical act of writing my book.

And I never forgot the first guidance she gave me. "Just write!" Once when the sadness and fear of COVID overwhelmed me, I remembered something I had read in Anne Lamott's book, *Bird by Bird* about paying attention, moving forward step by step. For now, all I had to do was keep writing, quit judging, focus on getting everything out of my head, and then continue organizing my story into coherent and compelling chapters.

And so, whenever I slowed down and started losing my momentum, I would take a walk, remember Lynya's guidance, and return renewed with words, wisdom, and especially, passion.

My stress would dissipate. I would be able to move forward, stay in the present, and feel a sense of peace. The words would start flowing once again.

DID YOU HAVE A TARGET AUDIENCE IN MIND WHEN YOU FIRST STARTED WRITING?

Through the years, as I dreamed of writing my book, I always thought the audience would be my age. As I grew older, so did my target audience. And that aging audience was growing older and smaller. When I finished my first draft, I asked Pat, a member of my Page Turners book club, "Will my only audience be women my age?"

"No," Pat answered. "Just think of all the others who will be inspired by your story. I think younger women will read your book and be inspired to make the time to travel with their mothers. Grandparents will love reading about your walking relationships with each of your grandsons. I'll bet if there is anyone who has been dreaming about hiking the Grand Canyon, they will read your book and decide to go for it. I think your descriptions of how you and Arnie communicated and supported each other will inspire husbands and wives who want to live satisfying lives together and apart in retirement. Your audience is much larger than you think."

I kept writing, editing, and receiving feedback. My target audience continued to expand. Not just women in their mid-forties who might get a late start with an active lifestyle. But also, younger women who might want to walk with their children or who wanted to inspire their mothers. Older women who might be inspired to get out and walk every day. People with joint replacement surgeries who learn they don't have to stop. They can keep moving forward and continue to capture their dreams. My audience kept growing as I wrote my memoir, shared it, and started receiving feedback.

Each review, text, email, and note was a gift. Each personal encounter warmed my heart.

Just a few days ago, I received this email from Makayla, my swimming coach who, in just three lessons had helped me realize that my core and style were strong enough to swim the crawl. I just had to get back in the pool and practice, practice, practice since I was starting from scratch after not swimming since the pandemic. Of course, I had given her a thank-you note and a copy of *Milepost 75*.

Hi, Sandi! I just finished reading your book and

WOW! I want to say thank you for writing this book. It's truly amazing and so inspiring. I have always wanted to hike the AT or at least part of it, and just felt it was out of reach, but you have taught me a valuable lesson and that is nothing is out of reach, ever. We just need to be determined to try and always be prepared with snacks!! I feel so honored to have met you and be a part of your trail journeys. I have shared the book with my whole family and can't wait for my mother to read it. Thank you. Thank you. Thank you, Ms. Sandi. You are an amazing, strong, and inspiring woman.

I read that sweet email. Took a big breath and smiled. I did not imagine or expect such touching feedback from young people as well as old when I first started writing. Pat was right. My target audience was much bigger than I realized.

WHY DID IT TAKE YOU SO LONG TO WRITE YOUR BOOK?

Before I answer this question, let me remind you I was never in a hurry.

My writing saga was divided into two periods of time. At first, I worked mainly with Lynya, along with an abundance of help from family and friends who became my alpha-readers and cheerleaders, from fall 2018 to fall 2022.

During that time, I followed Lynya's advice and kept writing almost every day, but I did not have a deadline. I was retired, in control of my time, and determined to enjoy the journey

My writing approach paralleled my event-walking approach. When I participated in events, I did not focus on winning, ignoring everything along the way, and keeping my eye on the finish line.

I simply enjoyed being outside, savoring the sights, stopping to take pictures, and sharing time with friends, other walkers, and volunteers. Writing my book was the same. I was elated to finally embark on this journey and was content to just keep moving forward. With joy, most of the time—except for those times when I got too judgy or worried about the future—and with gratitude, always.

The second period began in winter 2022 when I worked mainly with Thea Rademacher, my publisher, and my assigned editor, Paul Fredrickson. They helped guide me through the editing process—enhancing the flow, identifying themes and threads, making my memoir more readable and relatable.

Paul quickly realized that I tended to hover on the happy side of the personality pendulum. So, by the time I wrote about challenging treks, especially my final Grand Canyon hike, I had simply erased my doubts, fears, and struggles.

"Go back to the trail," Paul said. "Remember how you felt when you slipped and banged against the rock, how you started losing your energy, how Rachel started worrying about you, how you started worrying about Rachel worrying about you. This hike was not a slam dunk! Dig deep, chip through your typical technicolor veneer, and expose those times when you struggled. Let your readers know how much you hurt. Allow them to share that pain with you."

So, with Paul's help, my memoir even became a bit of a page-turner so readers could hike by my side, feel my angst, and begin to wonder if I could go the distance.

A new posse of old friends and new colleagues became my beta readers. Now the focus was on drilling down, digging deep, resolving inconsistencies, highlighting typos, all those tiny nits that many of us kept missing and that would drive readers crazy if we didn't catch them.

As I think about, "Why Did it Take so Long?" here's another answer to that question. After I met Lynya and got unstuck, writing became a key part of most days; however, writing was never the most important thing in my life.

Time with family has always been my highest priority. Arnie and I spent precious time together, chatting, walking, going to doctor appointments, cooking, watching *Jeopardy!* as we ate dinner together. I talked on the phone with Rachel. I walked and played cards with Jonathan, Arnie, Flip, and Sam.

My fitness and health also ranked high on the list. I participated in ballet exercise and Tai Chi classes twice a week. Also, walked outside every day.

I volunteered at the St Augustine Lighthouse one afternoon a week and was involved in other community activities.

And since it was now 2019, I was making the most of my year-long 75th birthday celebration list of events and adventures. I participated in a half marathon, a 5K, and a charity stair climb in February alone, three more events in spring, a whole summer of training, and several other events plus my Grand Canyon hike at the end of the year.

I trained for each of these events. Then participated in them. Flying up and down the East Coast, across the country, and across the Atlantic. Not much time for sitting at the computer and writing my book in 2019.

But I was still jotting and gathering. Since Lynya was already coaching me to show rather than tell and to take readers along with me, I became more intentional in capturing the feeling and flavor of my excursions, events, and experiences. I noticed and documented the tastes, smells, sights, and sounds in my daily journaling. I researched using all my senses, imagining all the ways I could become a tour guide to my armchair-traveling readers, quickly transcribing notes especially at the end of each day.

And I continued my habit of saving itineraries and preparation emails that now could serve as sources of details and data I could include in my manuscript.

So, while I did not make significant progress sitting at the computer writing my book during 2019, I had recorded and gathered a great deal of timely, relevant reference material ready to add delightful details to my event and travel tales.

COVID-19 HIT IN 2020. HOW DID THAT AFFECT THE WRITING OF YOUR BOOK?

Once my 75th birthday year ended in December 2019, I still had some activities planned for 2020. I was looking forward to a change of pace; however, I did not want to slow down too much. I could see no medical reason to cut back significantly on my walking and training. Despite my doctor's fears, my hips, knees, and feet were working just fine.

So, I participated in several events and activities that mirrored my 2019 January and February lifestyle. I continued to volunteer at the St. Augustine Lighthouse, participate in Tai Chi and ballet exercise, and walk every day. I completed the American Lung Association "Fight for Air" stair climb with Flip and Lauren (along with support from Sam and Jonathan) and the Donna Half Marathon with Camino hiking buddies Cathy and Jane. I wrapped up February with another St. Augustine Lighthouse 5K joined by an expanded team of five walkers from my ballet exercise class. My 76th year was off to a great start. I was on a roll!

Then March 2020 hit. I hung in there for a few days after the Wednesday shutdown, clinging to life as I knew it. The life I wanted to continue. I went to ballet exercise Thursday morning, then volunteered at the Lighthouse that afternoon. *It can't be this bad. I'm sure we will be okay. I will be careful, but I don't want to shut down.*

I even went shopping the following Monday trying to maintain my sense of normalcy. But when I came home with bags of groceries, Arnie looked concerned, not even curious about my purchases. He helped me wipe down the grocery bags and contents and put everything away.

"Can we talk?" he asked. We sat in his office. Arnie looked sad, hesitant. "I know how much you enjoy shopping, being able to browse, make your own decisions in the moment. I've never asked you to restrict your lifestyle because of me, but I'm scared. The news keeps getting worse. Will you please stop going out shopping until they get a handle on this thing? Until it blows over?" The pain on Arnie's face was palpable.

I looked down, then up at him. "Oh, my goodness. Of course I will! I'm sorry you had to ask me and that I added to your stress. I should have been more cautious and sensitive. We will weather this storm together."

COVID-19 shut down our world. We hunkered as if our lives depended on it, because they did. Arnie was severely compromised. We could not risk his getting exposed and infected. We struggled as we heard about lives lost and other lives severely altered.

Our pain increased as the pandemic entered our community. We were grateful our family and most close friends were spared. We helped by sending contributions. We were fortunate because we could hunker and keep ourselves safe. And so, we made it work. We survived. We thrived.

At first, I struggled with and even grumbled about Instacart. I *hated* not being able to pick out our own produce, to walk down the aisles checking out the sales, greeting others.

But then, Arnie became our master Instacart shopper. He turned at-home shopping into an adventure. We tipped big. It felt good to support those who risked their health to shop for us so we could protect ours. We eventually got to the point where we enjoyed making our selections and figuring out the nuances (like checking "no substitutions") on the computer together.

We missed our family. But we made that work too. We

preferred text, email, and phone calls rather than FaceTime or Zoom, so that's how we stayed in contact especially with Rachel, Rob, Jonathan, and Andrew. Occasionally Jonathan, Lauren, Flip, and Sam would drive down and stand on the sidewalk so we could chat and take pictures.

Jonathan used his supply officer talents and provided essential support with shopping, searching, finding, and delivering the items we could not locate. He'd pile them on the sidewalk a safe distance from our front door, then step back and wave as we retrieved them. We took pictures of each other to send to the rest of our family.

Arnie and I were determined to make the best of our new reality and to stay safe. We adjusted and adapted. I took long walks alone. We took short walks together.

We started taking selfies on our walks and sending them to the kids so they could see our smiles and be reassured we were doing just fine. I collected a portfolio of happy-walking selfies. At the time I did not realize how precious those pictures would become.

During those early months, we did not leave our home for anything other than our walks. So, we enhanced our lives in new ways. Playing Scrabble. Spending more time exercising on our in-home machines (his Nustep, my stationary bicycle), cooking delicious meals together (with food delivered by Instacart).

And I had much more time to write.

Usually, I'd start each day with a short walk to warm my muscles and fill my head with energy and ideas. Then I'd write at least 90 minutes each morning. After lunch, I'd take a short reading/relaxing/snoozing horizontal break. I'd get up, take a longer walk, stretch my legs, fill my heart with natural beauty and my head with new ideas. These walking breaks frequently helped me resolve writing issues and answer questions.

While I walked, I'd frequently play my own personal word game trying to remember key ideas that kept popping in my head by using mnemonics, challenging myself to rely on my head rather than my phone. For example, I might remember something Arnie told me (A), another benefit of walking (W), and maybe another sweet story about hiking the Great Wall in China (C). So, I would hold up my fingers and repeat, WAC, WAC, then rush to my office when I got home to write down the words so I would not forget them. It was a goofy approach, but it kept me entertained and stimulated. Then when I sat down to write the next time, I could include them in my manuscript.

Occasionally, especially in the afternoon, I would plan to write for one or two hours but would end up writing three, sometimes even four. Time flew. I would walk out of my office, shaking my head, telling Arnie, "That was *so* much fun!"

His usual response was, "I'm so happy for you." Unless it was starting to run into our cooking and eating-in-front-of-the-TV time.

I remember one time when I couldn't figure out how to describe my first WDW marathon along with depicting my journey from my despair with Florida humidity to the delight of discovering Florida beauty and bountiful walking spaces. I wrote and deleted. Tried again. Got majorly frustrated and then, of course, my anxiety ramped up.

So, I pulled up my big girl panties, put on my shoes, waved to Arnie, "Goodbye, I love you. Going out to clear my head," and headed out to walk and have a good talk with myself. *Get a grip! Your Orlando journey from adjusting to humidity to embarking on your Disney Marathon adventures is worthy and worth sharing. You can inspire others to find walking joy in every space they encounter. You can help readers learn to embrace walker-friendly marathons even when they are older. Find your voice. Tell your story!*

I walked, listened to my head-talk, the fog cleared, and it dawned on me how I could structure the chapter with flashbacks while I participated in my first Walt Disney World Marathon.

Ideas kept popping.

I turned around, rushed home, "Hi hon! I'm heading to my computer. My head is filled."

Arnie smiled, "Go for it!" I sat down. Got started. Words flowed. The sun dropped. My eyes stayed glued to the screen. My fingers typed furiously. I was in the zone. Time flew. I blinked and looked up. It was dark.

I tore out of my office. "Arnie! I'm so sorry. You must be starving."

He laughed, "Absolutely not. I snacked and then started dinner. I checked in on you a few times to make sure you were still alive. You were hunched over and typing away. There was no way I was tempted to disturb you, even to turn on your light. And now you're done. So, let's eat."

Arnie was by my side during my writing journey. Cheering my every word, sentence, page, chapter of progress. And occasionally cooking dinner when I lost track of time.

By the end of 2020, Arnie and I were alive and well.

And, I had finished my entire manuscript rough draft, almost 130,000 words.

 **HOW DID YOUR WRITING PROCESS CHANGE IN 2021?**

Lynya and I spent most of 2021 crisscrossing chapters back and forth. I'd address the edits Lynya sent, then email the chapter back to her while she was editing other chapters I'd already written and revised.

She kept prodding, pushing me to be more focused and precise. "How does this relate to your purpose? Do you really need that story? Remember, this is your memoir, your story. It's a memoir, not an autobiography. You don't have to include everything that happened. You are in control of your own story."

She pointed out potential inconsistencies. "When you describe the route on the One Day Hike, the apostrophes of White's Ferry and Harpers Ferry are not consistent. Please research and make sure these are correct." I checked and the apostrophe inconsistencies were correct. White's Ferry retained the possessive based on the name of one of the original owners. Harpers Ferry lost its apostrophe when in 1891 the United States Board on Geographic Names eliminated it. A little bit of research helped ensure apostrophe accuracy and add to my historical knowledge of the Chesapeake and Ohio Canal Towpath.

She urged me to dig deeper, "Create a stronger beginning to this chapter. You're getting closer, now stick your ending! Write a more powerful conclusion." She praised me when I nailed it. Gave me gold stars. Gave me bronze stars when she thought I could do better. More feedback. Big and small. My writing improved. My confidence increased. I had much to learn, but I was moving in the right direction.

Whenever I got stuck, most of the time a short walk along the ICW (Intracoastal Waterway) would clear my head. Occasionally I would write something and then sleep on it. My brain would process and often I would wake up in the middle of the night with precisely the words I wanted to use. I kept a notebook and pen by my bed, but usually I got out of bed and went to my office to document my thoughts. I knew I had to write them immediately or they would surely be lost by morning. After racking my brain one morning searching for a fabulous idea that had popped up and I had not written down during the night, I made a little sign for my nightstand with the Chinese proverb: "The strongest memory is weaker than the palest ink." No matter how tired I was, I never trusted my brain to remember something that occurred to me during the night. I had to write it down.

As I moved forward, navigating my writing path, sometimes I'd use little tricks to open my mind. I'd intentionally think about a scene I planned to write the next day just before turning out the lamp on my nightstand. It gave my brain something to work on during the night while I rested.

There were a few times when this approach backfired. When my brain would go into overdrive with so many ideas that even after I captured them, I could not go back to sleep. But most of the time, I slept well and when I opened my eyes the next morning, I could see the words, patiently waiting for me to get up and start writing them down.

Also, I am easily amused. For example, I even got a kick out of my Word program greeting me each time I opened my document with its hearty "Welcome back!"

At the end of 2021 my manuscript was in much better shape. Not a finished product but significantly improved. Most of the time, I thoroughly enjoyed the editing process.

I loved learning from Lynya. I also appreciated my own editing. It was fun to read my words and then discover even better ones. I was grateful I had come this far and was learning so much.

Just like boots were made for walking, I discovered my mind was made for writing.

 HOW DID YOU COME UP WITH YOUR TITLE?

I love telling this story! *Milepost 75* seems like the perfect title now, but coming up with just the right title was quite a process. When we came close to wrapping up the first draft, Lynya said, "For your next assignment, I want you to make a list of at least 100 titles. Whatever pops into your head. Just write, write, write until you can't think of anymore. Then come back the next day and write some more."

Really? But what did I know? She was my teacher. I was the student. So, I wrote, wrote, wrote. And wrote some more until I came up with a list of 110 titles.

You may think this was overkill. I certainly thought so at first. But the more titles I listed, the more I understood what was happening. Not only was I coming up with a title, but also, I was clarifying my purpose one more time. What did my book stand for? What was most important? What would entice people to read my book?

I had already learned from my reading and researching that most books had short, catchy titles: *Grandma Gatewood's Walk, Rim to River, Almost Somewhere.* But Lynya told me not to limit myself. She said short titles were fine, but she wanted me to write long ones too. I wrote titles the same way I wrote my manuscript. Just kept writing until there were no titles left in my head.

It was slow going at first. Not really trusting the process. I started with a few long titles like, *One More Year in My Adventure Land,* as I thought about all I wanted to do during the year I turned 75. Then I focused on my big hike scheduled for the end of the year, my Grand Canyon rim-to-rim, the hike that had eluded me for so many years. I jotted down a few titles like *One More Year - One Really Long Day,* and, *Turning 75 and Taking a Hike.*

Then the titles started flowing. I began having fun. I added, *Celebrating 75 with Trips, Trails, Trees and Tribe* as I remember-ed all my family hikes and adventures. I reflected on the times when it made sense to delay, wait until next year, but then deciding to forge ahead. *Year-Long Journey Through 75 - It's Now or Never*

The list got longer. I started including the word "milestone." *Milestone 75: Life, List, Lessons, and Love,* or *Making the Most of Milestone 75.* When I hit 100 titles I decided to add a few more just for good measure. I finally stopped at 110.

Then the real work started. Picking the best one. Lynya and I bounced our favorites back and forth. I finally landed on *Milepost 75. What a perfect title for my first book! I can just keep writing books as I move through the years. Milepost 80. Milepost 85. Who knows how far I'll be able to go! And I can even use Milepost, plus my age, for many of my chapter headings.*

As I look back on this list, it strikes me the words mile post did not show up until number 95, and that Milepost 75 did not show up until number 106. I also remember thinking *Ahah!* when I wrote that title. *Sandi, that's it. It's not really a milestone although I'm celebrating a milestone birthday of 75. It's a milepost!* That word rebounded and resonated as I thought of all my hikes when I relied on those precious mileposts to let me know how far I had come and how much farther I needed to go. They motivated me. Each post, especially when they were placed at each mile along the trail or road, reminded me that I just had to keep going until the next milepost. Mile by mile. Step by step. And so, I reached the finish line with my title!

My memoir had a first name. Good enough for now. I could work on the last name later.

And just for fun, you can see my long list of title ideas in Appendix B of this book!

HOW WERE YOU ABLE TO REMEMBER SO MUCH DETAIL?

I still had all those journals I had written through the years. Many times, they helped refresh my memory. I just didn't let them bog me down the way I had before I met Lynya. If I wanted to check on one detail, I'd do a quick check and get back to writing. If the source wasn't readily available, to avoid going down a rabbit hole searching for the right journal, I would jot a note to myself on a post it and search for it later in the day.

In some cases, I printed and saved emails and texts that described certain situations, usually ones I sent to the kids, describing a medical issue, or new happy encounter along the trail, or at the St Augustine Lighthouse. Even a few of my Facebook posts came in handy.

Then I put all my journals and travel memorabilia in a small box on a table right by my desk so I had just one place to look.

I labeled a set of manilla folders with chapter numbers and headings and placed them in the same box. If I came across an old email or something else relevant, I'd print it and toss it in the appropriate chapter file.

But, the most amazing thing is, there were many times when I would sit down, begin typing, and the memories would pop up! It was almost like a movie started playing in my head. It was a crystal-clear picture of what I remembered. I would watch my *mind movie* for a while; then start typing, trying to keep up with the dialogue playing in my head. Time would fly. At this point, I rarely edited. I often rambled as I tried to keep up with all the thoughts and memories. I was surprised at how, as I typed, the scene would continue to unfold with dialogue, sights, sounds, sometimes even tastes and smells.

These were *my* memories. They weren't always correct. When Rachel and Jonathan read what I wrote, there were times they set me straight. In one case, Rachel had to remind me of all the caring options she offered when I told her I had made our North Rim lodging reservations for the right dates and wrong year.

Another time, Jonathan said, "Mom! I would never say anything like 'it was beyond my wildest dreams,'" when we were discussing our trip to China. Oh. He was right!

I appreciated their help, happily corrected my story to fit their memories, and moved on.

I think the best gift I gave myself was that since this was *my* memoir and *my* recollections, not every reflection had to be perfect. I adjusted when I received corrections, like from the kids, but I gave myself some latitude and grace. The information in my memoir was simply to the best of my knowledge.

 ## HOW DID YOU DEAL WITH WRITER'S BLOCK?

I don't remember ever being blocked. Stalled a few times but never blocked. Maybe, because I had this book in my head for so many years, the words just kept coming and my fingers had to rush to keep up. When my memories would fade, I'd be patient, knowing the right words would eventually seep into my brain. If I felt bogged down, I'd move on to another chapter, another topic. There were so many storylines that needed to be filled in. I always found some place to continue writing.

After my short morning walk, many times my head would be so filled with good ideas, as soon as I got home, I'd grab my journal and jot down all my notes before I'd forget them. Then after chatting with Arnie and getting settled, I would sit down at the computer and the ideas were right there, noted in my journal, waiting for me. I just had to keep writing.

There *were* times I'd struggle with how to write about a sensitive topic. For example, while I had absolutely no problem sharing most of my health issues, when it came to the sensitive topic of my urinary incontinence, I initially struggled.

And Arnie struggled too. He did *not* want people to know his health was failing, that he was on oxygen, that he needed a walker. He was happy to share his story with individuals we saw in person who asked about his portable oxygen machine, especially if he could help others to obtain a machine that would help them get out and about, but whenever we took family pictures, especially if we planned to post them on Facebook, he insisted on removing his nosepiece.

I understood how he felt. He did not want to be defined or remembered by his oxygen nosepiece or walking aid. He was so much more than that. It would be like me wearing a T-shirt saying, "I pee a lot!!" on every Facebook family photo.

Although I had shared my incontinence issues with family and friends, it would be intimidating to include it in my book for everyone to read. I initially hesitated. Having to pee a lot is so personal and private!

But then I remembered a woman I met when Arnie and I first moved to Palm Coast who said she no longer walked on any of the beautiful paths surrounding Palm Coast. She was afraid to walk too far because she had to pee so often. She looked sad. Like she had lost something. And she had. The joy of walking!

That's why I included my personal story. I figured if I could help just a few women seek options rather than simply stop walking, it would be worth that possible embarrassment for me.

Since I was becoming more active as Arnie was slowing down, I needed to find a way to communicate that in a sensitive and caring way, one that he would be comfortable with, that would preserve his dignity.

I delayed including information regarding his health issues for most of 2021, but it sat in the back of my mind. I knew how hard he was trying. I also saw how his health was declining. This was my memoir. I could determine what stories I included. But Arnie's frail and fading health did have an impact on me and our lives going forward, especially after I retired. And, as I wrote about how he and I had worked together to make the best of our ascending and descending health trajectories, it helped me get to gratitude. We were partners. I helped him. He celebrated me. Both of us supported each other in the best way we could.

Finally, after walking with this writing challenge lodged in my head and then sleeping on it, I decided to include a brief sentence in Chapter 8: "Climbing High: Again." When I wrote the section about our discussion about my post-retirement plans, I could explain that Arnie had slowed down due to medical problems, and that was why he was concerned that I'd speed up so much I would not have time for him. Arnie read the comment I had inserted. He smiled and gave me a thumbs up.

Dealing with my writer's stall regarding health and aging ended up being a worthwhile and worthy benefit of my writing journey. It was another opportunity to build trust between me and Arnie. It was another example of what it truly meant to be together "in sickness and in health."

It made good sense to pause and consider the difference this book could make in my life and in others.

 DID YOU JOIN A WRITERS' GROUP?

No, I did not join a writers' group. I was already a member of Page Turners, a book club that ended up being the perfect group for me. We were all avid readers. At the time, I was the only writer.

It took me a while to get far enough along with my memoir to admit to my group that I was writing a book. We all knew of others who talked about writing a book but never managed to get around to completing it and getting it published. I did not want to be one of those people. I could not ask them to believe in me and then let them down. What if I didn't finish? What if it's bad? What if I give up? What if I can't get it published? What if my friends get bored? It was like admitting I was going to hike the Inca Trail when I had no idea if I could do it.

Although I still wasn't totally confident I would go the distance, there came a time when I built up the courage to tell them. I knew them well. I trusted them to believe in me and believe I'd get it done.

When I finally admitted to them—I think sometime in 2021— that I was writing a book, they immediately adopted me as their resident author. They encouraged me. They held me accountable. Our leader, Peg, put me on the monthly meeting agenda, "Progress updates from Sandi." Now that certainly helped keep me on track!

They were patient. They stayed curious. At each meeting they'd digest my updates, ask for more details, then share my joy as I learned more about the ins and outs and ups and downs of my writing journey.

They even understood when I told them my publisher and I had decided to push back the publication date from the end of 2023 to the beginning of 2024 so it wouldn't get smothered in all the big holiday releases. Also, I was still waiting for a few more responses to my requests for blurbs.

We dissected my writing and publishing process with the same discipline we applied to our book club approach. We selected monthly books that were interesting, often challenging. Although we used a portion of our meeting to share personal updates, we dedicated most of our time to discussing the book. Asking and answering questions about writing style. Characters. Plots. Insights. Would we recommend to others? Why or why not? Even though we weren't reading my book at the time, I was learning even more about writing a good book by reading and discussing good books. What resonated with this group of discerning readers? What kept them turning the pages?

I stayed with this reading group long after I moved to Jacksonville, building relationships, reading fascinating books, and continuing to grow closer. Some of us met for lunch before our meetings. We started emailing each other with personal updates and stories.

This dear book club became a community of friends sharing support that extended far beyond the covers of a book.

SINCE YOU WEREN'T IN A WRITERS' GROUP, HOW DID YOU OBTAIN FEEDBACK ON YOUR WRITING?

I asked almost every person I named in *Milepost 75* to read their portion just to make sure they were satisfied with how I had portrayed them, if I had made any mistakes, if they had anything to adjust or add. Several of those friends asked if they could read the rest of my manuscript. As *Milepost 75* grew and I told more friends about it, more of them volunteered to read it. I asked them to respond to a few basic questions Lynya had created for me.

Please let me know:

> When you were bored.
> When you were confused.
> When you wanted to read more.
> When you wanted to read less.

Early on, I needed big picture general feedback. "I know it will be hard to ignore, but please don't spend time correcting typos, grammar, or punctuation. This is a rough draft. We will drill down on those details later in the proof-editing process."

As my manuscript grew, I hesitated to ask my friends to continue reading, but several insisted. They said they were hooked. They wanted to join me for the entire journey. A few ignored my guidance and scrutinized every page, making notes, providing detailed feedback. Several people who barely knew me volunteered to read my entire manuscript! "Are you sure?" I asked Pat, a Page Turner member. "It's so big, bulky, and long."

She smiled, "Yes, I'm sure. I have enjoyed listening to your updates. I'm curious and excited. I'm happy to be a part of your writing journey and I want to help you any way I can." She joined a growing group of people who read all or a portion of my early, rough manuscript.

These readers were caring and candid. Thank goodness! In many cases they confirmed the feedback Lynya had already given me. I had listened to most of her feedback but resisted making a few of the changes she had recommended. But in many cases, my readers agreed with Lynya, and so I complied and made the changes. When I admitted this to Lynya, she chuckled.

My readers were caring and candid. Thank goodness for their honesty. They told me when they were confused. They also asked me to provide more information when they didn't understand something. In one case, Kathie told me she had to look up at least ten references in my chapter about Israel. I used words familiar to me, but foreign to her. I needed this kind of feedback!

They told me which stories they loved, that resonated, like the ones about sharing adventures with my family and the times I struggled with physical issues, failures, and often self-doubt. They especially appreciated reading how Arnie and I came to an understanding about my traveling while he stayed at home. They were touched by the many ways he supported and encouraged me. Always urging me on. Never holding me back. Some readers did not know Arnie very well, but after reading my book, they certainly knew about how well he treated me.

They also highlighted sections that inspired them and told me that they had already changed their behavior based on what they had read. One friend emailed, "I decided to manage my retirement savings differently since I read how you were spending the kids' inheritance now so you could enjoy it together while you're still alive. That sounds like a great strategy. Thank you!"

My early-reader team embraced me and my manuscript. They kept me moving forward through my initial writing and editing process. They helped me make my memoir more relatable, readable, understandable, and engaging.

DID YOUR WRITING IMPROVE AS YOU WROTE YOUR BOOK?

Absolutely! I did not attend any formal writing classes, but my writing improved through writing, receiving feedback, and coaching—and reading.

I read. A lot.

Best sellers. Non-best sellers. Books published by big publishing houses. Books published by small local firms. Books that were self-published.

As I read, I chatted with each author in my head. "Why did you include that story?" "That is so clever!" "Maybe I can use your approach."

I read each author's acknowledgements, marveling at all the support they received, all the people they thanked. And when I finished reading the entire book, I thanked the author for all they did to entertain, educate, and encourage me.

I made it a point to read every book I could find written by senior hikers, especially women. Many of these books were self-published, so that helped me see firsthand the pluses and minuses of that approach. I was pleased and encouraged to see so many well-written self-published books. Clearly, there were many authors who knew how to publish their own material and do it well.

I reread several of the classic books on writing. *Bird by Bird* by Anne Lamott kept me writing and smiling. She keeps me going today as I read her articles about aging. *Writing Down the Bones* by Natalie Goldberg helped build my confidence and encouraged my combination of walking and writing—the physicality of movement and meditation. She, too, helped me embrace my bad first drafts. *The Art of Memoir* by Mary Carr helped me see my memoir as a piece of art that was beautiful to me and even to others. Her book empowered me to write my story.

These books still nestle in my nightstand, tabbed, creased, and underlined, ready to be of service whenever needed.

I also read *Elderhood: Redefining Aging, Transforming Medicine, Reimagining Life* by Louise Aronson and *Aging Wisely: Facing Emotional Challenges from 50 to 85+ Years* by Viola Mecke. These books helped me more accurately understand and describe what was going on in my own aging body and psyche. Later, I discovered sharing my struggles with others helped them keep moving forward even when it became harder, and we were all getting slower.

We elders can learn from each other. We can hold hands, hug each other, lean together, learn together.

These books also increased my awareness and gratitude for all the decisions I had made earlier in my life to stay healthy for today and maybe more importantly, tomorrow.

Of course, I reread *Grandma Gatewood's Walk,* the story of Emma Gatewood's improbable and unstoppable hike along the entire Appalachian Trail. She became to the first woman to solo hike the trail at age 67, relying on her gumption and the help of others. This book, published in 2014, was meaningful in many ways. Arnie gave me my first copy for my 71st birthday. He signed it, "Thank you for taking such incredible care of me! Love, Arnie." He loved me so well. He knew how much I would appreciate and even need this book. Emma inspired me. She just kept moving forward no matter what.

Her story inspired me to keep walking, pushing myself to find new places to walk and train in and around our new neighborhood when we moved to Palm Coast, Florida the year after I retired. When we met new neighbors, one of the first questions I would ask was, "Are there any hiking trails nearby?"

Finally, the third neighbor I asked gave me my answer, "Oh, yes. It's right down at the end of our block. The Intracoastal Waterway Esplanade. And if that isn't long enough for you, you can walk down the street at the end of the esplanade and pick up the trail that leads to Waterfront Park and another trail along the Intracoastal Waterway."

I reread *Grandma Gatewood's Walk* shortly after I started writing my book to learn how the author, Ben Montgomery, organized his book. How he told Emma's story. How he started and ended each chapter. It was like taking a master class in hiking and walking—old woman style. I underlined. I tabbed. It served as another reference book.

I became an even more voracious reader of hikes, walks, big adventures and small. I read several books on hiking the Camino de Santiago. My favorite was *Walking with Sam*, the *New York Times* bestselling travel memoir by Andrew McCarthy about his long hike with his son, Sam. My Grand Canyon hikes with Rachel and my Great Wall hike with Jonathan and Flip echoed some of McCarthy's experiences with his son. I learned a great deal from Andrew's writing style and his story telling about family and the Camino. Another master teacher.

I was frustrated that I could not find any books about shorter hikes along the Camino de Santiago written by, say, an old lady who had the time and capacity to hike just a portion. I had searched for such a book when I was training for our Sarria to Santiago hike (Chapter 14: "Hiking the Way – My Way"). Later, that famous quote from Toni Morrison popped up on my phone, "If there's a book that you want to read, but it hasn't been written yet, then you must write it." It was then that I decided to include a longer chapter about our hike on the Camino, figuring that there were many other hikers like us who might be interested in learning more about that shorter hike and the value of embracing a portion of the whole.

I read these books the way I've always read books, with pen in hand, bending page corners, circling lyrical phrases and words.

Even before I started writing my book, I always circled new words and wrote them in a spiral notebook so I could review them and incorporate them into my speaking vocabulary. And now I had the opportunity to include a few of them in my writing. I remember looking up and learning the word *quotidian* and learning it meant "ordinary, or every day, especially when mundane." I did not use that word in my manuscript, but I sure do like the sound of that word. I did use new words like *detritus* and *ennui*.

And then, there's *cacophony*.

"Mom, you love the word cacophony, don't you?" Rachel said after reading my book. I could hear the smile in her voice.

"Oh no, did I use it too much?"

"Well, I saw it at least three times."

"Yikes. Yes. I do love it, but I will get rid of two of them. Thanks!" So, I replaced cacophonies with words like clamor, blaring, or simply noisy.

Later, I told Thea my story and she burst out laughing. "Oh, Sandi, you are not alone. Authors love that word! I'll bet you can't find a memoir that doesn't include cacophony at least once. So, you're in good company."

And this should be no big surprise: I am a slow, plodding reader. Especially since I started writing *Milepost 75*. I don't simply read books, I study them.

I also read book reviews. Especially reviews of books in my genre, learning what readers liked.

Readers appreciated being inspired by captivating flow and compelling descriptions. Five-star reviews often included words like "page-turner," "unable to put this down," "I fell in love at hello with this character," "This writing style lifted me up." Many reviews were written as beautifully as the books the readers had reviewed!

I also learned early on what readers didn't like. Typos, poor grammar, and clumsy repetitions were guaranteed to generate low-star reviews.

Reading reviews also motivated me to write more reviews myself. I enjoyed being able to support other authors. And it made me smile to see my words in print, even in the review of another author's book.

Readers seemed to gravitate toward books that focused on a single trail or journey like the Appalachian Trail or John Muir Trail. I worried my book would not be quite as compelling since I included stories about many trails, not just one. Although I started and ended my memoir with Grand Canyon hikes, I didn't highlight those hikes in my title. I also included several others like the Inca Trail in Peru and the Sierra Club One Day Hike 50K along the Chesapeake and Ohio Canal Towpath.

This was my story. And it felt good to write it. I accepted this would not be a perfect book, a bestseller on the caliber of *Grandma Gatewood*, but I was learning, improving, and starting to believe *Milepost 75* could be a well-written and worthy book that would engage and delight readers. And that would be good enough.

HOW MUCH EDITING DID YOU DO AFTER YOUR FIRST DRAFT?

All I can say is it's a good thing I did not fall in love with my words because by the end of the entire process I had to cut almost 50,000 words. My first draft was around 130,000 words. I knew I had to cut! Some of the cutting was hard, but mostly I found my initial editing process satisfying and delightful. I'd read a sentence. *Wait. I can rephrase this to make it even better! I can make this more concise and compelling.* I discovered redundancies and better ways to articulate. As I edited, my writing became more entertaining and engaging. My editing days were usually filled with joy. And since I was not under any kind of self-imposed timeline, I gave myself all the time I needed to make the best of this process.

Lynya provided valuable guidance. I was surprised at how many times my repetitions and redundancies watered down my writing making it sloggy instead of splashy.

I heard Stephen King say in an interview on *CBS News Sunday Morning*, "I write for myself. I edit for my readers."

Thank you for that writing lesson, Stephen King! As I edited, I'd think about how much my readers would appreciate my new, improved, and streamlined writing.

When it came time to cut out some stories—even those I really liked—Lynya reminded me, "You're not killing your stories, you're just moving them to a holding area for now." And that's what both she and I did, keeping copies of the original manuscript and highlighting the stories that had been cut. I figured, someday, they might come in handy. I could use them in blogs, or maybe podcasts. Perhaps they could be included in my next book.

After months of editing with Lynya, we had whittled my manuscript from 130,000 to 108,00 words. My memoir was more concise and readable, and still needed more work.

PART II

My Path to Publishing

HOW DID YOU SECURE A PUBLISHER?

This is another story that reinforces my caveat that this is not a how-to book. It's my personal story, precious and unique.

My publishing story started when I received an email from lifelong friend, Lynn Murphy, announcing the publication of her new book, *50 Life Lessons from Inspiring Women*. She was asking for help in promoting it.

I immediately responded. "Congratulations! I just ordered a copy and will help spread the word. Did you self-publish?"

Lynn immediately replied, "No. I have a fabulous publisher, Thea Rademacher, president of Flint Hills Publishing. I could not have done it without her. Do you have a publisher? Would you like an introduction to Thea?"

I was stunned. Overwhelmed. Lynn was offering me the opportunity to connect with her publisher. I thanked her profusely and told her that I wanted to wait until I finished editing my manuscript before making the connection.

What an incredible gift. Having this opportunity gave me a path forward. But even then, I did not take anything for granted. I told Arnie, "Even if Thea does not want to accept my manuscript, maybe she might know another publisher I could reach out to." I embraced that hope. Sent a loving hug to Lynn. And started editing my manuscript one more time with even more fervor.

And I thanked the universe for the confluence of connections with dear friends, serendipity, timing, and luck.

But securing a publisher was just one step.

Other setbacks loomed ahead.

My life had been filled with stories of never giving up, mostly associated with growing older and dealing with body breakdowns. In all cases, even with joint replacements of hips and knees, broken feet, and atrial fibrillation, I slowed down, started over, but never gave up. I was used to dealing with and overcoming physical issues. I'd had lots of practice.

But it had been quite a while since I had dealt with the loss of a dear family member. My mom had died many years ago. My brother, Chuck, had also died just before the world shut down due to COVID-19. I still felt the pain of their absence in my life.

Then, during the fall of 2022 just when I had started drafting my query letter to Thea, Arnie, my dear husband of almost 54 years died, unexpectedly, in the hospital. His heart stopped beating with no warning. I never got to say goodbye.

His health had been failing for several years, but the doctors were discussing discharge. Rachel, Jonathan, and I were making plans to take him home and get him started on rehab. We were stunned and numb as we went through the process of dealing with his death rather than planning for home health care.

I was stopped cold. It was hard enough to get up each morning, even eat, much less even think about moving forward with my book.

Rachel and Jonathan helped me deal with my grief as they grappled with their own. I could not go home and sleep in the same bed Arnie and I shared, so they removed our big bed and replaced it with a smaller one for me to sleep in, alone.

Rachel stayed with me for a few more days when I was finally able to move into our ... my empty home after camping out on Jonathan's couch for a week. I still struggled. I was stuck even though I knew full well Arnie would want me to move forward. I walked a little. I ate a little. I sat staring into space a lot. I couldn't imagine my life without him. I was broken. The echoes of his laughter and chatter were deafening. The silence oppressive.

I decided to fly to Maryland to stay at our tiny cabin and spend weekends with Rachel, Rob, and Andrew, who lived just 25 minutes away. It was hard to be alone at the cabin, but this was Arnie's happy place. I needed to spend some time here, alone, with Arnie. At first, it was hard. Every room echoed. The loss of his presence shrouded everything.

Then, little by little, memories of his joyful spirit made the air a bit lighter. It became easier to breathe. I was surrounded by Arnie, his clothes, a little bowl filled with pens, many things that made him happy, especially his comfy recliner and giant fire pit.

I raked leaves. Burned them in his pit, sat and watched the flames shooting high in the sky, dancing, waving at me, reminding me of Arnie's glee as he basked in their glow. It would be the first of many moments that would release some grief in my heart and replace it with joy. Sometimes, as I sat there, I would even find myself smiling.

The process of reading and writing also aided my healing. I sat at our kitchen table and reread all the sympathy cards the kids and I had received. Our dear friends and family shared their sweet memories of Arnie. He would have loved all the stories and recollections. These heartwarming words written by those who knew and appreciated Arnie made such a difference. I wrote thank-you notes, responding to every card, contribution, and acknowledgement of his life well lived.

One afternoon shortly after I finished writing my final thank-you note, I stood up, walked into the bedroom and saw one of Arnie's socks that had fallen on the floor. I collapsed on the bed and started sobbing. Wailing. I curled up in a ball. Still broken. So alone. Unable to fathom life without Arnie. I fell into an exhausted sleep. Later, in that space between sleeping and waking, I remembered our last conversation. Arnie and I were alone in the ICU. It was just a few days before his heart stopped. "I'm so sorry I didn't take better care of myself. That I'm putting you through this," he said, his voice soft and sad.

I stood by the railing of his bed, leaned over, and locked eyes with him. "You have *nothing* to apologize for! It has been an honor to care for you. You cared for me, making my life possible, filling it with kindness and joy. And now, even here, you treat everyone with such grace, gratitude, and humor. You never gave up. You always kept trying. You're uncomfortable, stuck in this hospital, and still, you are a kind and patient, patient. You still make others laugh. You make me laugh. I love you so much."

I stared hard. He needed to know how much I loved him and what a good person he was. That he had nothing to apologize for. He stared back, gave a little nod, blinked his eyes, cracked a tiny smile. This was our moment.

We just didn't know it would be our last.

Now I was fully awake. I *had* been able to say goodbye to Arnie. I just didn't realize it at the time. I flipped over my tear-soaked pillow and fell back into a gentle sleep.

After a few more days of rambling around the cabin gradually healing and feeling grateful, I went back outside to rake a few more leaves and start another fire. The flames shot into the air. Smoke danced with the flames, then floated high. I sat and pictured Arnie relaxing in his special chair watching his fire in his firepit. He was smiling. Content. Blissful. He turned from the fire, looked at me, and nodded, "Hon, it's time to move forward."

He was right. It was time for me to call my dear friend Lynn Murphy about taking her up on her offer to introduce me to her publisher, Thea Rademacher.

"Lynn, I want to finish writing my query letter and do one more review of my manuscript so I can get everything sent to Thea a few weeks before Christmas."

Lynn responded, "I don't think you have to rush to get this in. Thea just told me she's swamped with work. She may not even have time to look at anything from you right now. I am so glad you're finally ready to meet her. You will love her. She's a feminist and huge women's rights advocate. She's an attorney who used to handle domestic violence cases. Let me give her a call and I'll get back to you."

A few days later an email from Lynn to me and Thea popped up on my computer:

Sandi,

Our long, and long-overdue, conversation was such a pleasure.

I talked to Thea as promised. I'm introducing you two with this email so you can schedule a conversation and start talking about your manuscript and getting to know each other. I've told Thea about you, our long friendship, and the fascinating story you've crafted.

She is not ready for you to submit by December 9th, the date you thought you might have it ready, so that pressure is off. She will tell you she has numerous projects to kick off the first of the year that will keep her from devoting the time she'd like to your manuscript. When you talk to her, you two can decide a workable target date. She can also share her thoughts during your conversation.

I know you two will hit it off, and I'm delighted that Thea will consider publishing your book.

I'll leave it to you two to figure out the next steps.

I could hear Arnie's laughter. "Told you so. Leave it up to Lynn to make things happen!"

Arnie's spirit helped me move forward in my writing journey.

And my writing journey helped me keep going after Arnie died.

Thea and I emailed. We set a call date. Then I panicked and started obsessively planning for the call. Writing detailed notes. Lists of questions. Things I wanted her to know about me and my book. Making myself crazy.

I wrote the following script I thought I might use:

Thea, thank you for talking with me today before you have even seen my manuscript. I'd like to make best use of our time, especially yours, so how much time have you allotted for this call?

I'd like to learn a little more about you.

Can I tell you a bit about my manuscript and why I think you would want to publish it

Finally, I have some publishing questions based on your book *Authors Beware*. Why did you decide to become a publisher? What delights you about serving authors in this capacity? How do you define a successful venture/collaboration?

I had even written out a small vignette as an example of how my life story inspires people:

A few weeks ago, I headed out in the last wave of the Richmond VA 8K (5 miles). In previous years, I had walked the half marathon, but I had neither the spirit nor strength to do it this year. I was still dealing with the grief of losing Arnie. I was also struggling severe spinal stenosis pain. I was even slower than usual. I struggled.

I was alone. With just a few people behind me. And I was in the slowest wave! My mind was buzzing. *Why am I doing this? I could have waved goodbye to Rachel and Rob when they headed out on the half marathon and just strolled over to the finish line to cheer for them when they crossed. I'm not sure I can do this.*

Then I looked ahead and saw a woman ahead of me who had a great pace. My mind calmed down. There was hope ahead. *If I can just keep up with her, I should be able to complete this 8K in a reasonable time, maybe even under two hours.*

I walked a little faster, caught up with her. We walked side-by-side for a minute or so. She looked over and said, "Hi! You have a great pace. Do you want to walk together? This is my first event ever and I'm scared. I don't know what to expect."

Talk about music to my ears! We ended up walking the entire distance. I explained the route to her. She told me about her husband waiting for her at the end and their plans to walk an upcoming half marathon together after they trained harder.

I told her about Arnie, that we had been married for almost 54 years, and my gratitude for all the goodness in our lives.

She turned. "Almost 54 years? How old *are* you?"

"I'm 78."

"You're 78. And you're still walking in events? I'm 58. I thought we were about the same age."

We spent most of the rest of the walk with her peppering me with questions about how I managed to stay fit and how she could be me in 20 years.

Time flew. So did our feet. And we crossed the finish line in 1.5 hours. In high spirits. Feeling strong.

I planned to wrap up my sales pitch to Thea with, "I look forward to meeting with book clubs to tell my story, answer their questions, and share their stories. I will encourage them to get started moving forward if they're stalled so we can win this aging game together."

I was prepped and ready to learn all I could about Thea, and to make my pitch.

Thea called. I took a deep breath. Organized my list of topics and questions. Sat up straight. We introduced ourselves. I laughed, "I am sitting here with pages of notes. I think I over-prepared."

Thea laughed, "That's music to my ears. I think I'd enjoy working with you." She then went on to tell me about her history, how she got started, why she got started, and why she believed in supporting emerging authors. Memoirs are her favorite. She explained that Flint Hill Publishing was a family business with her husband, Steve, as CFO, and her sons as editors. She answered most of my questions before I asked them. As our time came to an end, she said, "Lynn told me all about you and your book. I usually don't talk to authors before I review their manuscript but, in this case, I trusted Lynn's judgement and I'm delighted we talked. Please send me your manuscript and I will let you know by the end of the year if I will accept it."

I was confused. She couldn't see me cocking my head, squinting my eyes. After a brief pause, "Okay. Thanks! I'll send my manuscript right away. Uhm. Should I also send my query letter?"

"No need Sandi. This call was your query letter!"

I sent the manuscript to Thea and tried to put it out of my mind. What would happen, would happen.

Now I could get back to spending my mind and walking time going through the healing process with my kids. I moved out of the cabin and stayed with Rachel, Rob, and Andrew through Thanksgiving. Rachel and I walked and talked. Sharing our favorite memories. Healing together.

After I returned to Jacksonville, Jonathan and I walked, shared our memories. Healing with each footstep.

I also walked alone. But never totally. When I headed out to walk on December 1, 2022, celebrating what would have been our 54th anniversary, Arnie joined me. I felt his loving spirit by my side. We had been married for almost 54 years. We had raised two beautiful children. We had struggled at first as children of divorced moms with slight, scattered memories of our fathers and scant understanding of how a good marriage was supposed to work. But we figured it out. We made it work for us. Ours was a good marriage.

And as I looked ahead, the fog began to clear, and a path appeared. I began to see a picture of my life without Arnie. My grief would remain. I would still feel pain when I check "widow" instead of "married." I would still feel broken, not completely whole. But my life would not be empty. I would not be alone.

I felt our children, Rachel and Jonathan walking on either side of me, each holding my hand, sharing their love, giving me strength, reassuring me we would cherish our memories, cook his favorite recipes, keep full-family traditions alive. Our entire family, children, grandchildren, and in-laws would stay connected for the love of Arnie and for the sake of keeping our lives filled with joy.

And if you're curious, you can find a copy of the query letter I didn't have to send to Thea at the back of this book, Appendix C.

WHAT WAS IT LIKE TO WORK WITH A NEW EDITOR?

It was a different and exciting experience from the very beginning.

Thea accepted my manuscript at the end of the year and scheduled a call mid-January 2023 with the three of us: me, Thea, and Paul, her 23-year-old son, my new editor. "Sandi meet Paul. Paul meet Sandi. This should be a perfect partnership. This will be Paul's first editing assignment. Sandi, this is your first book. Paul is an author. He knows how to edit. Your book will be in good hands. I know the two of you will enjoy working together."

She continued, "Before the two of you get to know each other, here are a few editing decisions I've already made. Sandi, I know you won't like this, but we need to remove all the direct quotes you had included at the start of each chapter. These quotes are beautiful and relevant, but to keep them in your book you will need to seek permission from each quote's author. This is time consuming, and I don't believe there is that much added value. This story is about you, not the quotes. We also need to remove song lyrics. Yes, they are beautiful and relevant, but you can paraphrase. I'm strict about this. We don't want to get bogged down. Our goal is to avoid any legal issues."

Thea continued, "And you will need to trim down your word count to around 80,000 words. Even 80,000 is long for a memoir by an unknown author but I think we can work with that.

"I'm relieved you're not in a rush and don't have a hard deadline. You've told me you have some trips planned this year and so does Paul. If we stay on course, we should be able to get your book published late this year or early next. We can get this done and you and Paul can still honor your other plans. Okay, Paul? You go ahead and tell Sandi how you plan to work with her."

Paul said, "Sandi, I read your manuscript from beginning to end. It's a great story and I look forward to working with you. I've already highlighted sections we can cut, but I want to assure you we will discuss and agree on each of these sections. Ultimately, it's your book and your decision regarding what stays in and what is removed.

"As we both know, part of our job will be to work together to trim almost 30,000 words from your memoir. I'm sure that sounds daunting to you, but it will be even more challenging when I tell you there are several areas in your story where you need to add more. To fill in details. To get to the heart of what you've reported. There are many instances where you can help the reader be right there with you, not standing off to the side. After our call, I will send you the first few chapters I've edited, and then you and I can schedule a Zoom call so we can discuss and make changes in real time. How does that sound?"

"It sounds great. Thank you, Thea for accepting my manuscript and for assigning Paul as my editor. Thank you, Paul, for all the time and thought you have already dedicated to my book. I love that you are the same age as Jonathan, my oldest grandson, and I look forward to working with you."

Thea and Paul helped me prepare for a new adventure. We were off to a great start.

WHAT WAS THE DIFFERENCE BETWEEN WORKING WITH YOUR WRITING COACH AND YOUR NEW EDITOR?

Both Lynya and Paul taught me how to become a more proficient writer. They helped me improve my style, sentence structure, and especially storytelling.

They were two different people with different goals and perspectives at different points in my life and different stages of my book.

Lynya began her work with me with a blank slate. She helped me create something from nothing. One of her biggest jobs, as I think back, was to encourage me to keep writing, do a brain dump of all those stories in my head. She helped me create the skeleton of my book, and then start filling it in, making it come alive. Once my book started taking shape, she helped me tighten my chapters with strong beginnings and endings. She worked with me to stick to my purpose in each chapter.

She helped me get started, get my story out of my head, helped get it organized and remove the areas that distracted from the point of my book. She coached, guided, and suggested. There were times I pushed back on a good decision of hers only to have some of my alpha-readers give me the same feedback. Then I'd go back to Lynya with, "Okay, you were right. Let's make that change." And she would chuckle.

Paul started with a written story. Everything was finally out of my head. At least I thought it was. He worked with a hefty manuscript that had to be trimmed down and tightened up.

Lynya helped me get everything written in chapters,

following an outline, telling my story. Paul helped me expose the layer of feelings below the surface. He helped me make my writing more heartfelt, touching, and lyrical.

In a way, the difference in working with Lynya and Paul was like the difference between alpha readers and beta readers. First, with Lynya, the big picture, flow, clarity. Second, with Paul, deep finesse, fine tuning, and detail. More creative constraints on word count. More opportunity to engage and invite readers to join me as I mourned a loss, healed from a surgery, struggled on a trail, or celebrated when I reached an elusive goal.

I needed both, and with their help, I achieved my goal of writing my memoir.

 HOW DID YOU AND PAUL WORK TOGETHER?

Paul sent me his edits on the first three chapters as he had promised, and we scheduled a Zoom call to discuss and make changes in real time. The timing was perfect. I had returned to the cabin after enjoying three months in Jacksonville. Jonathan and I had walked in the preserve near my home almost every morning. We continued to savor precious moments talking, walking, and healing together. Then, later in March I flew back to Maryland to our cabin. Rachel and Rob arranged for one of them or Andrew to pick me up Thursday afternoon so I could spend Friday, Saturday, and Sunday with them. They would take me back to the cabin Sunday afternoon and I would treat Monday through Thursday as my alone/editing/healing time.

I was in a beautiful, creative setting. When I needed a break, I would walk or, even better, rake some leaves, start a fire, and spend some time enjoying memories of Arnie's joy in this peaceful place. Then I would get back to my computer that rested on the kitchen table in front of a large window that looked out to the firepit and forest.

It was my own little writer's retreat.

As Paul promised, he sent detailed notes along with his edits of the first three chapters. He shared his writing approach and philosophy. Although I did not agree with a few of the cuts he had suggested, I already appreciated his intelligent, incisive, and inclusive approach.

We quickly established a pattern in our Zoom-call meetings, sharing personal updates, general questions and reactions, and then getting down to detail. We both knew I was nervous about losing big swaths of my story. I worried they had to be cut because they really weren't that good.

On our first call, Paul reassured me. "Sandi, let me give you just one example of some material I thoroughly enjoyed that we will still have to cut. Let's take your chapter on Madrid. I'm going to ask you to cut most of it because it's not directly relevant to your story of hiking the Camino de Santiago. I loved reading about the art in the Prado and Sofia Reyna, but I think we should mainly focus on your search for *Guernica* and how that iconic painting brought back those precious memories of you and Arnie when you saw *Guernica* in MOMA in New York the first year you were married.

"I also found myself smiling with delight as you, Jane, and Cathy searched for and finally found the statue of the Bear and the Strawberry Tree in Puerta del Sol. You included the history and vividly described the festival atmosphere of that iconic town square. But we need to cut it from this memoir. You never know, maybe at some point you could write a separate book that includes descriptions of all the art you have discovered on your trips."

That's what we proceeded to do. We trimmed large sections. Paul also helped me identify repetitions and redundancies. I thought Lynya and I had removed them all, but they still lurked, adding more words that muddied my story. He was my teacher and colleague. We worked together to make my memoir more readable. To make every page and every word count.

He helped me recognize several topics that tied the chapters together. Themes I had not recognized. He helped me highlight those themes, using them as threads to tighten my story and make seamless connections across the years and chapters of my memoir. For example, he pointed out the link between the shiny dimes I tossed on the trail to motivate Rachel on our long walks when she was young, to the moment at the bottom of the Grand Canyon when she motivated me by pointing out the silver suspension bridge across the Colorado River.

Paul also shared his talent and expertise as a poet and teacher. He highlighted sections that could be more whimsical, giving a beat to my footsteps, making my tale even more delightful for me to write and my readers to read.

Then Paul gave me the best editing gift of all. "Sandi, there are few poignant pieces of your story that you simply report rather than digging deep into what was going on in your head and heart and how you were able to deal with that hurt, loss, and pain. The first example is when you describe your mother's death. You wrote that she died in 1995, and you quickly moved on to the next topic. I know you were conscious of word count, but her death must have been devastating for you. How did you deal with that loss? Especially because she seemed so strong and healthy. How were you able to move forward? We must trim words from your manuscript, but you still need to share the full story with your readers. Describe that pain. Let your readers feel how it felt. Allow them to join you, walk in your shoes as you take the steps to heal from that loss. I'd like for you to take the next few weeks to think about losing your mom. Write that story."

I listened to Paul and took the time to reflect and remember how broken I felt. The terrible pain. The times I would start to cry for no reason. Especially when I couldn't call her. Ask her a question about my childhood. I thought about the baby steps I took to move forward. The little ways I honored her memory. My favorite ritual became tossing a rock into the water at Bridge Number 5 at on the tram route at Sabino Canyon. Watching the ripples. Remembering her delight when she, Rachel, and I rode the tram to celebrate her 79th birthday, the last one she celebrated.

What I didn't realize until I started writing this current book, is how much working with Paul, editing the manuscript I wrote while Arnie was still alive, had helped me heal from his death. I'd read a chapter and remember how much Arnie was with me in body as I wrote at home during COVID-19. How much he was by my side in spirit as I traveled far and wide. And how he was still by my side in poignant memories during the entire editing process.

Writing *Milepost 75* helped me keep Arnie alive. Not just for me, but for our family and friends. But especially for me. As I edited and reflected, his tangible support in my life became even more vivid. We were such a good team. I am so grateful for our life together. And I'm especially grateful I was able to capture so much of our loving relationship in my book.

Paul helped me improve my writing. He also helped me heal.

HOW DID YOU COME UP WITH THE REST OF YOUR TITLE?

Well, I can assure you, I did not write a list of 100 sub-titles. However, I did make a small list of possibilities including the following:

> *Milepost 75: Why Turning 75 was One of the Best Birthdays Yet!*
> *Milepost 75: Not Your Typical Old Lady...*
> *Milepost 75: The Wonders of Life at 75*
> *Milepost 75: The Joys and Tribulations of Turning and Celebrating 75*

Milepost 75: Aging Adventurously – Climbing, Walking, Hiking, Living, and Loving Every Step of the Way

This time, the list just wasn't working for me. I even tried *An Ode to the Miles, Moments, and Memories for my 75th Year*, but at the end of my book-writing journey, I realized it was much more than simply my 75th-year odyssey. It was also about never giving up. Taking risks and leaning into courage and curiosity. Hurting and healing. And most of all, love and support.

Paul and I had finished our edits. We were almost ready to send it to Thea. We wanted to get this done, but we also wanted to get the full title just right. We played a little more with "Aging Adventurously" and "Hiking, Living, Loving."

"Paul, I think it's more than just hiking. I got it. *Exploring*! That includes every adventure—traveling, investigating, learning, even climbing flights of stairs in a long, dark stairwell."

We kept bouncing ideas back and forth. "I think the title needs something about the setbacks. My surgeries and injuries. My failures to complete. I think that might resonate with readers. Maybe *resilience*? I like that word."

And finally, I realized especially as I wrote my book that I could not have done this without Arnie. He made this life possible. He had my back and was by my side the entire distance. So, I knew the last word in my title would have to be "love."

"Good job, Sandi. We're getting closer," Paul emailed.

It came to me that night. I got up and wrote in down…of course. The next morning, I emailed Paul, "I think I've got it. What do you think?" *Milepost 75: Aging and Exploring Life Trails with Wonder, Resilience, and Love.*

Paul's email sailed back, "Perfect!"

My memoir finally had a first and last name!

WHAT WERE SOME OF THE ADVANTAGES OF WORKING WITH A PUBLISHER?

I had no idea what it would be like to work with a publisher. This was new territory. I felt so fortunate. I knew Thea would publish my book and provide editing resources. I also knew I would pay an upfront fee, which I did. Half when we signed the contract and the other half when my book was published. I expected to pay 8-10K. It was lower than I expected.

The huge bonus in working with Thea was not only was she a publisher, but also, she was a lawyer. She had written the book, literally. Her *Authors Beware! Arm Yourself with Knowledge to Help Avoid Legal Pitfalls* was filled with vital facts that would inform, advise, and protect authors. I received the best of the best. Thea was a caring and consciousness publisher who knew all there was to know about the legal issues associated with publishing a book. How fortuitous!

No surprise, Thea's contract was very detailed. It precisely addressed her responsibilities and mine. What was covered in my fee and what was not covered. What I could expect in every step of the process.

Also, in working with Thea and Flint Hills Publishing, I became a member of the FHP community of authors. We met each other through Zoom classes, interviews, and book launches. Some of us created stronger bonds. We encouraged each other and read each other's books. This connection with other FHP authors turned into a gift that keeps on giving. Two authors wrote blurbs for *Milepost 75*. Another author guided me through the process of requesting blurbs. We continue to celebrate and support each other as we move forward on our writing journeys.

Also, through Thea, I had access to thoughtful, talented, creative, and reasonably-priced resources. Greg German became my patient and encouraging technical support person who created the spectacular website that told my *Milepost 75* story with a lovely array of photos, excerpts, and accolades. Greg is a poet and world traveler. We enjoyed getting to know each other. Sharing travel stories. He embraced my book and encouraged me. He even came up with my domain name—*milepoststories*.

Another talented resource, Traci Osborn, created the stunning collage artwork for my front and back book covers. Thea, herself, did the book formatting for production. Her dear husband and FHP CFO, Steve, provided valuable assistance on all things financial. I was surrounded by a team filled with talent, goodness, and grace. I was in good hands.

Thea also created valuable promotional tools for me. She designed a bookmark that included a picture of my brilliant and eye-catching *Milepost 75* book cover on the front. And sure enough, people's eyes lit up when I gave one to them. It was just a bookmark, but folks seemed delighted. She used the back to include my head shot, and this lovely summary: "*Milepost 75* is an inspiring memoir about aging adventurously. Through many challenges including having both hips and knees replaced, Sandra shows us the value of moving forward, not just on the hiking trail, but life's paths as well."

Just a few days ago, I handed one to the receptionist when I checked in for my appointment with my primary care physician. When I returned to check out, she said, "I had time to read your bookmark and guess what? I have an artificial hip and will have both knees replaced later this year. We have a lot in common. I'm going to buy your book!" We exchanged emails and she promised to keep me updated on her surgeries.

My bookmarks create connections. They have become my calling card. (You can see my bookmark at Appendix D.)

Thea also crafted an insert for all those books I was giving away. It urged readers to help get the word out. I especially appreciate that she included a request to post honest reviews on Amazon. I have learned that getting reviews can help educate potential readers and create additional sales of my book, but it's a struggle. As she stated, "Marketing a book takes a ton of GRIT!" Her kind message with her little nudge may help. (The graphic of the insert is included as Appendix E. You are welcome to modify it for your own book!)

Because Thea is a lifelong learner, she provided venues for the authors in the Flint Hills Publishing community to learn along with her. She hosted Zoom seminars on podcasting, creating audio books, marketing, and one of my big priorities, obtaining blurbs. Although writing a book can be a solitary process, I was now a member of a brand-new community. The Flint Hills Publishing community.

Working with Thea provided many more resources and opportunities than all the services listed in her contract. Our relationship continues to grow deeper. She is not only my publisher; she is also my dear friend.

YOUR BLURBS ARE GREAT! HOW DID YOU MANAGE TO GET SO MANY?

Thank you! For as long as I can remember, I have enjoyed reading the blurbs on the back cover and front pages of books. I wondered how authors were able to solicit and secure these. I hoped I would be able to obtain some blurbs for my book. I did more than hope. I set my dream goal of obtaining ten blurbs.

After Paul and I finished editing my manuscript, I read articles on requesting blurbs. One of the key and consistent recommendations was to use the first paragraph of my request to create a strong link with the person I was contacting. To share what I know and appreciate about this person. To share a compelling reason why this person might be willing to read my manuscript and write a blurb.

Then, I received a huge infusion of support and assistance from Thea. Of course! Fortuitously, she hosted a Zoom class on—*tada!*—"How to Request Blurbs!" She used this session to interview one of her Flint Hills Publishing authors, Clyde Toland, who had obtained an impressive number of blurbs for his recent biography of Medal of Honor recipient, Major General Frederick Funston. Clyde shared his approach and urged us to give it a try. His mantra was, "It never hurts to ask." And to put a monumental exclamation mark on that mantra, he followed up with, "I even received a blurb from General David Petraeus!"

Clyde made it sound so easy. But it wasn't. Reading a book and writing a blurb is a tall task. It was hard enough to ask my friends and colleagues, but asking a total stranger? That seemed too overwhelming. So, I eased my way into it. First, I made a blurb-request list of people I knew. Then I added people whose writing I admired, people who had influenced and delighted me through their stories and books. If I hesitated to put a name on my list, especially the name of a famous author, I just remembered Clyde's words, "There's no downside. Just ask. You'll never know if you don't."

I kept learning by reading articles on requesting blurbs. The first guideline stated in every article, and shared by Clyde, was to make a connection with the author. "Let the author know you have invested time in them. You have read their writing. You appreciate their writing." I still struggled. So, I decided to go one step further. My plan was to attach a PDF of the manuscript to my email and follow up with mailing an Advance Review Copy (ARC) just to make it easy and comfortable for them to read. Then, to top it all off, I created a photo collage for each individual author with pictures of their book covers and a statement of admiration for their writing. I attached the collage to card stock and included a note referring to my email and again requesting a blurb. I decided to leave no stone unturned.

Since Clyde asked us to contact him with any questions, I

emailed a draft of my first request to him asking if he would review and give me some feedback. Of course he did, in his typical, gentle way. He made a few word edits and then followed with the following recommendation:

> *I suggest the following paragraph in place of your next to the last paragraph:*
> "After reading the above information, I hope that you will be willing to write a blurb for my book. If so, please email your blurb to me by November 15. If you prefer not to write a blurb for any reason, I will understand."
> *Proposed new last paragraph:*
> "Thank you very much for your serious consideration of my request. My best wishes to you as you move forward with your exciting, active, inspirational life."
> *There is no way to know how any recipient will respond to any given letter. Thus, you do the best that you can and keep your fingers crossed! Good luck.*

I did the best I could, sent the following blurb request to someone I had never met, Tom Zoellner, author of *Rim to River: Looking into the Heart of Arizona*, and crossed my fingers:

Dear Tom,

I know you because I attended your presentation at the 2023 Tucson Festival of Books. I initially assumed your book was about hiking the Grand Canyon Rim to River and even brought along the May 1992 *Arizona Highways* with the article about my first attempt at hiking the rim-to-rim-to-rim with my 15-year-old daughter. But as I listened to your presentation, you got me hooked on the Arizona Trail! I sat in the front asking questions, dreaming of thru hiking someday—knowing

I probably wouldn't—but at least adding it to my list of day-hike dreams.

Then I read your book. I was delighted it told the story of your hike and the back story of so many things that happened in the Arizona that comprised 50 years of my life from 1948 to 1998. As you hiked closer to Tucson and then the southern border, I stayed up late reading, needing to know how it ended, also wanting to re-connect with so many places that were part of my life. And I loved reading about your parents. How they met you along the way and supported you.

So, with this extremely tangential bond of sitting in your presentation and reading your book, I'm going to forge ahead and ask you to read the attached PDF or advanced reader copy of my book *Milepost 75* (in the mail) and write a blurb. The rest of this letter will include some reasons to encourage you to grant this audacious request.

I am a late starter at almost everything. My active lifestyle (45), finishing school (53), adventure travel that started shortly after I retired at 70, and even writing my first book. (Due to be published in early 2024, the year I turn 80.)

My memoir provides an opportunity for arm-chair travelers to share in other adventures both here and abroad, including, the Inca Trail in Peru, the Sierra Club-sponsored One Day Hike 50K along the Chesapeake & Ohio Canal Towpath, Great Wall 8.5K "fun run," Petra, Israel, even a few Walt Disney World Marathons. All slow, steady, and walker friendly. I've never ever been a runner. Don't win or place first. I usually finish at the end of most events, a solid member of the "back-pack."

Milepost 75 is filled with snippets of

walking/hiking/climbing experiences with every member of my family including kids, grandkids, in-laws, brother, cousin, also friends. My beloved husband Arnie provided loving support across the miles through our daily calls.

This might be just the right time for people to read my story especially given what we learned about health and longevity during COVID. Many of those who survived, even thrived, were the ones who stayed happily, actively fit in very ordinary ways. I walked every day throughout the *hunkering* months. Not far or fast. Just out and walking, which I still do today even though I have four artificial joints, arthritic feet, spinal stenosis, and atrial fibrillation.

Thank you very much for your serious consideration of my request. My best wishes to you as you move forward with your exciting, active, inspirational life.

Sandra Richmond

This was Tom's initial response:

Hi Sandra,

I'd be pleased to look at this for possible cover comment. Send me a reminder if you haven't heard from me by Xmas? And congratulations! To finish in the back of the pack is to finish with honor, if you ask me.

Ditat Deus, Tom

And this was Tom's blurb response:

Hi Sandra,

I read your book and am pleased to provide the following endorsement:

"In *Milepost 75*, Sandra Richmond describes a life

full of purpose, friendship, and physical adventure that doesn't involve chasing championships but rather the simple pleasures of experiencing the world in motion, even with four artificial joints and a late start in the world of endurance hikes and marathons. To finish in the middle of the pack, or even dragging up last, is to finish with honor. We can all learn from Sandra's example."

–Tom Zoellner, author of *Rim to River: Looking into the Heart of Arizona*

Let me know if this works? And congratulations, not just for the book but for what was described in the book.

With admiration,
Tom

The following year, I met Tom at the 2024 Tucson Festival of Books. My friend, Fuzzy, a classmate from my first University of Arizona master's degree program, served as a volunteer at the authors' lounge. She told me to stop by and she would ask Tom to come out to meet me. Lynn and I met Fuzzy at the door, she went into the lounge and came out with Tom.

He greeted me with a big smile, shaking his head as we shook hands. "So, how old are you now? Are you still hiking the Grand Canyon?" Then he turned to Lynn and said, "She even sent me a specially created photo-collage card with a hand-written note."

Milepost 75 wasn't published yet. But I had my copy of his book and asked him to sign it. Which he did.

For Sandi,
A fellow traveler of Arizona's roads, trails, and byways. I am so happy to have been given your excellent writing. Keep it up far beyond *Milepost 75*!

With all my best, and Ditat Deus, Tom

We posed for a picture. Then he introduced me to another author. "This is Sandi Richmond. But I'm giving her the trail name of *Canyon Rat*. She has earned that name. Even though we have never hiked together, we became hiking partners when I read her book."

Now—that is a great blurb story!!

In some cases, I did not receive a response. Some thanked me and said they would not write a blurb, but even these responses were thoughtful and encouraging. My favorite came from Barbara Kingsolver's office:

Dear Ms. Richmond,

Thank you for writing to Barbara Kingsolver about your memoir *Milepost 75*. She is so honored that you hold her opinion in such regard and thought to reach out to her. Unfortunately, her office receives more manuscripts than she can possibly read. They all look compelling, and it is difficult to choose among them. As such, she has decided to step out of the jacket blurb economy, as the requests have become far too numerous.

That being said, it was so lovely to read about your background and story. Barbara would encourage you to keep writing and continue loving the place you are from. (My link to Barbara was that she wrote about many places in Arizona where I lived.) Thank you also for such kind words about her work. Please know that Barbara wishes you the very best.

Wow! What a beautiful "turndown." I have read every one of Barbara Kingsolver's books and will continue to do so, appreciating her brilliant writing and now also, her warm and encouraging thoughtfulness.

While, as Clyde advised, "It never hurts to ask and there is no downside," I discovered that in most cases, the blurbs I received were written by people with whom I had a link, either personal, from my publisher, or through good friends. Although two authors with whom I had absolutely no links except that I had read and enjoyed their books, Tom Zoellner and Chris Crowley, did respond and wrote lovely blurbs. So, Clyde was right—it never hurts to ask

I sent out twenty requests and received ten blurbs. Requesting those twenty blurbs was time consuming. It was also expensive since I mailed ARCs with every request. But for me it was a worthy and worthwhile investment. I received thoughtful and beautiful blurbs, many of them accompanied with heart-warming encouragement.

For example, Joseph Grenny responded with, "Congratulations on the book! It looks like a very worthy project and I'm sure will bless lives."

Chris Crowley added to his blurb email, "I am impressed by what you have done, and you write well, which is rarer than you might think."

Melissa Bowersock and I did not know each other, but a mutual friend suggested I ask her to write a blurb. She not only wrote a heartwarming blurb, she helped with proof editing my entire book. She also sent this heartfelt message, "Your book touched me and made me cry at points. The emotion was palpable. I think it's great that you're going to give presentations of the book. I'm sure it will help others."

Melissa had already self-published more than 50 books. She also shared marketing ideas with me. As we emailed back and forth, we learned we had much in common, especially that we were both recent widows. We described those moments when daily experiences caused a new sense of loss. I told her about my bittersweet feelings when I finally learned to work the label maker to create the labels I made for my 5X7 photo albums. This used to be Arnie's job. I was happy I could now manage this by myself, but sad that it was one more task I could perform without Arnie's assistance. I was losing him one task at a time. Melissa shared a similar story about making a decision regarding car maintenance, something her late husband, Bud, always handled. We named ourselves "grief sisters."

Ten generous people took their precious time to send me beautiful blurbs. They also helped me believe my book was well written and worthy; that it might make a difference. My community expanded. My blurb journey enhanced my book and enriched my life.

It never hurts to ask. I'm so glad I did.

YOU'VE TALKED ABOUT HOW YOU MADE SUBSTANTIAL CUTS TO YOUR EARLY DRAFTS. HOW DID YOU DECIDE WHAT TO REMOVE?

I don't have a single answer to this question. Deciding what to remove happened at different times and in a variety of ways. For example, the first example I've included below was a last-minute coda to Chapter 14 "Hiking the Way – My Way," the Camino de Santiago chapter. I had added it to my original manuscript just as I was getting ready to start reviewing and removing stories, trying to trim back my word count. As I think back, there may have even been a fatigue factor. At this point, I just wanted to get this process finished. Maybe, for the first time, I was getting impatient. The Camino chapter already felt too long. I didn't want to break it into two chapters, so I decided on my own to remove this story even though it had just recently dawned on me how much more the Camino hike had enriched my life than I initially realized.

Learning about "supported hikes" opened a whole new world for me. Before Camino, I had felt guilty and wimpy because I did not want to backpack. I felt limited, restricted by my own weakness. Not quite good enough or strong enough as those hearty souls who carried their own heavy pack.

When I learned that multi-day hikes are made possible by others doing the heavy lifting, it changed my life.

CAMINO LESSONS – 488 words

Here I thought I was so active-travel smart. How could I have missed this?

I knew about tours, long one-day hikes, cruises, treks. But until Camino, I did not know that many businesses specialize in transporting luggage from one stop to the next, so hikers carry just the few things they'll need in a daypack.

What a discovery! I could hike for many days in a row and not carry a heavy backpack.

Up until Camino I had figured I knew just about everything about making trips easier and adventures bigger, but I really *hadn't* traveled that much and clearly had much more to learn.

I had always felt like a bit of an outlier in that I didn't like lugging backpacks for camping along the trail on long hikes. I knew about the folks who hiked the Appalachian Trail (AT) or Pacific Crest Trail (PCT) with bulky bags on their muscled backs. I admired their strength and endurance—even their balance—to carry so much weight and still walk straight. But since that was not for me, I had limited myself to hikes that could be completed in one day or less. I loved the freedom of hiking unburdened and free moving. Grand Canyon hikes and the One Day Hike were my mainstay. One day. My way.

Hiking Camino opened the door to a new vista of future travel and hiking opportunities that I could add to my limited repertoire of backpack-free day-long hikes.

Macs Adventure and many other travel companies provide assisted support for hiking long, multi-day trails in some places I never heard of. I read about a 10-day hike along the Hadrian's Wall Path, a National Trail stretching east-west across England. Never heard of this but it sure sounded interesting.

I embraced this new adventure option that supports many small businesses along the entire trail. I loved the model of lodging and dining in local towns and villages, having luggage transported from place to place, and hiking the distance in between each stop on my own pace.

I enjoyed my Israel tour group experience. I loved our Inca Trail guided trek. I would do more guided hikes like that, but now I had another opportunity to explore farther and walk longer.

The Camino was wide open, accessible to others who would not or could not hike down the Grand Canyon, up the Inca Trail, or across the AT. I remembered the people I met—the group of grandparents, the woman with her walker, the elderly man who decided that his Camino was one day long. So many new doors were opened on this trek. A whole new world.

I think I'm going to start doing more research about that Hadrian's Wall Path hike.

When I started working with Paul, we had to make even deeper cuts. Not one of these decisions was easy, but I kept thinking of my readers. I did not want them to be overwhelmed, impatient for the chapter to end, but rather looking forward to turning each page, as long as there weren't too many of them.

Paul and I decided to cut this next story near the end of my

Israel chapter because Sherry and I were on the last day of our trip. We were anxious to get home, and I suspected my readers might be ready to move on to the next chapter. I included this story for you to read simply because these many years later, it's still one of my favorite memories. Maybe even more poignant now. It was a different time back then. Even amid all the turmoil, there was a sense of relative calm and growing belief among many that peace might be possible.

ISRAEL – 275 words:

The next day we travel north back to Tel Aviv on the final day of our tour, still stopping and touring sites along the way. The most memorable stop for me is Kibbutz Sde Boker, the large campus that includes the retirement home of Israeli Prime Minister David Ben-Gurion and his wife, Paula.

Before reaching his home, the bus stops so we can visit the final resting place of the Ben-Gurions. We walk up a narrow dirt path bordered by lush trees that arch across the trail providing shade and sense of solemnity. Just before we reach the crest of the hill, we see a group of small slender ibex, a wild goat indigenous to this territory. I pause to absorb the beauty of this scene. My chest tightens, eyes well with tears. The history, peacefulness, not sure why, but it takes a few minutes to pull myself together. Maybe it's because this is our last day. Finally, I get going and catch up with the rest of the group. We reach the tombs, gaze across the Negev Desert, and feel a soft breeze.

It's a short ride to the Ben-Gurions' retirement home, a tiny hut, filled with books, mementos, and even a small table where he met with world leaders in this humble setting. The home, this setting, is a tribute to Ben-Gurion's leadership and humility. His zest for life is depicted by a bronze life-sized statue of him standing on his head. I stand for a picture, hold on to his foot, and say, "Thank you, dear prime minister, for your life well lived and your inspiration."

The following was a story in another chapter that was already too long. The point of Chapter 6: "Finding Balance on the Great Wall," focused mainly on my roles of mother and grandmother with Jonathan and Flip. I also wanted readers to enjoy some armchair traveling and learn a few more intimate aspects of my personal journeys. I included this story for a couple of reasons. First, it's a sweet tale of women helping women. And second, it's another example of being able to travel with urinary incontinence issues and even find joy in the process.

TIANANMEN SQUARE: 300 words

Jenny rejoined our smaller team. When she warned us there were only a few restrooms in the Forbidden City, that sounded an alarm for me, so I broke away from our group to find a bathroom. I was fully potty-trained from my trips to Peru, with a handful of toilet tissue in my right pocket and a small bottle of anti-bac in my left.

I searched. I found. The cavernous restroom was packed. Many of the stalls in the front were drop toilets which I had used before. Then I noticed some shorter lines of older women standing in front of the few stalls that had flushing toilets rather than holes which was my preference as trip fatigue enveloped me. I stood out, tall, Anglo, old, tired, trying to figure out how to slip through the crowd to get to those shorter lines near the rear of the room.

A woman looked up, saw the look in my eyes, and grabbed me around the waist with one arm. She pushed me along and spoke quickly to another woman who did the same. They passed me from one woman to another until I came to a flush-toilet stall that had just opened. The woman closest to the door nodded, smiled, and pushed me in.

I finished, came out, saying, "Xie xie, Xie xie." They smiled big, then one woman grabbed me, pushed me back though the crowd, handing me off to another as the next woman in line entered the stall. I made a quick exit, and walked back to my group, smiling.

One description of this scene could be a chaotic, claustrophobic collage of crowded China, but I will remember it as a very physical literally hands-on collegial connection of women helping women.

This next story was one of the toughest ones for me to cut. Jonathan and I walked many miles and events together throughout my writing years and beyond.

Because this was the final event on my 75th birthday list and because it was one of my favorite examples of how Jonathan helped lift me up and made me smile. I wanted it to stay in *Milepost 75*.

I accepted the candid and caring feedback regarding the arch of my memoir. That it should end with the Grand Canyon rim-to-rim. Sadly, I cut it. Now, happily, I include it here for you to read.

DECEMBER 2019 BULOW PARK
13.6 MILE TRAIL RUN: 1025 words

It came time for the final item on my 75th birthday list, the December 13.6-mile Bulow Park Trail Run with trail notes that ominously warned, "Please watch your footing carefully! There are sections that have numerous roots, areas that may be churned up by wildlife, muddy areas that are slippery, branches may be hanging down and scattered on the ground. Plan to get wet. Your pace will be slower. Plan to have a change of socks, at least, and possibly shoes at the finish line."

Jonathan and I had hiked this last year. We were slow. We did get wet. It was hard. We knew the drill and were delighted to do it again. What a spectacular way to wrap up my 75th birthday year.

Despite its dire trail notes I viewed Bulow State Park as a home to a series of bountiful, bough-filled, lumpy, bumpy trails. It is a place of marshy, marvelous natural diversity. The trail meanders through marshland and forest. It is a beautiful hike, filled with goodness and gnarly goop. Hard to hike and equally hard to resist. And the finisher medals are made of real-wood knotholes!

I was excited and unusually nervous. I needed a pep talk. *If I could hike the R2R, I should be able to do this. Right? No jet lag. It's half the distance of the Grand Canyon. No steep climbs. No elevation. It's Florida, land of the flat. It will be fine. I will be fine. I hope.*

Jonathan and I checked in and strolled over to greet our familiar favorite 400-year-old glorious and majestic Fairchild Oak Tree. This lovely beauty stands stately with her strong, sprawling branches covered with Spanish moss and other unfamiliar green, filmy garments. For a few moments we stood immersed in the spiritual sanctuary of this tree. We forgot about the trail and savored the serenity that only nature can provide.

Our peace was shattered by the blast of a horn and the announcement for the 50K ultra-marathoners to head out for their early start. We pinned on our bibs, took a last-minute potty stop, lined up at the rear of the half marathon wave and in front of the 4.25-mile wave.

The horn blew again, and it was time for us to hit the trail with no worries about our finish time since the event would be open extended hours for the 50K. We hiked with confidence as we stepped over smaller roots on the drier, wider section of the trail. For a short time, it was just us and a few other slow half marathoners. Then the wave of 4.25-mile runners roiled up and raced by as we stepped to the side of the narrow trail to let them power through. We moved back to the calm with just the few of us slower walkers playing leapfrog with each other as we gingerly straddled the palm fronds covering the puddles in the middle of the trail. We stopped to take pictures and survey the landscape as we approached the wider, dryer section of the trail with its scattered, statuesque trees and softly-waving bushes, brushes, and branches. We pointed out birds and critters, caught up on family news.

After the first 3.5 miles, we entered the narrow, muddy, precariously big-root lumpy section of the half marathon route where we walked single file stepping carefully over weaving roots that crisscrossed the trail.

Another hour passed. It got warmer. It grew darker as we walked deeper into the dense forest. The light from the sun was cut off by the overhead canopy of branches and leaves, but heavy heat still managed to filter through. We reached the turn-around rest stop and filled our water bottles. "Please grab some goodies. We have lots of fig newtons and trail mix," the volunteers urged.

We grabbed a few snacks then headed back on the same trail. Around Mile 10, I started to fade. The heat and humidity weighed on me like a wet blanket. Now we were both watching my step. Jonathan held my hand or offered his arm to help me climb up and over a few slippery, slimy bridges.

He walked ahead on the narrow path. The

inevitable concrete-like mud started accumulating on my shoes. *I will be fine. I have to be fine. I am fine. I think.* The roots started to shrink as they covered the trail in smaller, more intricate weaving patterns. The mud dried and flaked away from my shoes. The hardest part of the trail was behind me, but I still couldn't shake the fatigue.

Jonathan stopped in the middle of the trail and turned around, "Mom, are you okay? You've been quiet for quite a while."

"I'm fine. Just tired. And frustrated that I'm tired."

"Really, Mom? Really? You're frustrated because you're hot and tired after hiking almost 12 miles on this trail? I'm not even 40 and I'm hot and tired!

"I'm not surprised you're feeling weak, but I am surprised you're frustrated. You're my mom. You're always so positive. You're the one who gives pep talks! You know what? You're old. I'll give you a break. I will be the one to give us the pep talk this time."

Jonathan gave me one of his infectious grins, then looked serious, "I am proud of you. You are my inspiration, and I just keep hoping I can be as strong as you are when I'm your age. You are 75 and you're almost done with a 13.6-mile hike on a tough trail at the end of an amazing year. And to me it seems like you just keep getting stronger. So, buck up, lady, and embrace who you are and what you're able to accomplish. Okay?"

Jonathan nodded at his job well done, turned around, and headed out on the trail just a few steps ahead. I bucked up, sloughed off the wet blanket of doubt, and let my spirit soar as we step out of the dense forest and back into the bright, beautiful sunlight of the final section.

Being able to include these stories in this book makes me happy. And who knows what will happen in the future to some of the other stories that were not included in *Milepost 75*? What I know for sure is that I wrote them with love and even if nobody else ever reads them, they will stay in my heart and remain part of my life story.

DID WRITING THIS MEMOIR AND RECEIVING FEEDBACK CREATE A NEW PURPOSE FOR YOU?

Yes! Eventually, I did discover a new purpose through my writing and the feedback I received, but that took a while.

At first, I was delighted to see reviews posted on Amazon. I read and celebrated every comment, texting the kids, "I got another review!" Sometimes, Rachel and Jonathan found them first and texted me. It was an exciting time for all of us.

I had learned early on that Amazon reviews are valuable in terms of building credibility and even increasing sales. But more important to me was the feedback. What did readers like? What did they not like? What could I learn in terms of writing my next book? More immediately, what stories inspired readers that I could highlight in my book talks and meetings with book clubs?

An early review stated, "This book is a great read. I loved hearing about the author's life, life experience, and motivation to meet many of her goals through walking. Her grit and determination come through the pages. This honest look at staying fit while getting older, continuously challenging ourselves, and the power of friends, family, and those you meet along the way. A real story by a real person who tells it like it is. Thank you, Sandra!" This reader captured many of the themes I wanted to convey. I didn't know this reader, but I certainly appreciate their feedback. I was encouraged!

A few other reviews highlighted themes I had hoped would resonate with my readers, such as this one, "Sandi's resilience and true appreciation for the reward of dedication is both inspirational and motivational. Her *Milepost 75* is colorful, insightful, whimsical, emotionally raw at times, and incredibly heartwarming. Her writing style is delightfully informal and comfortable. Sandi offers an exquisite bird's eye view and perspective of what 'Trail Magic' really means, and she shares the beauty and depth of her family traditions. You will thoroughly enjoy reading this masterpiece, as you embrace this lovely reflection of Sandi's real life 'awesome journey' getting to her *Milepost 75.*"

How exciting! Readers were responding to my stories and lessons. They were highlighting parts of my journey that were also important to me.

This next review was labeled "The Joy of Being." "I so enjoyed reading about Sandi's walking adventures in far and not so faraway places. Her grit and determination is inspirational. Her love of family is heartwarming and evident throughout her memoir." This reader *got* my focus on family!

And this reader surprised me with her specific recommendation, "Ms Richmond's memoir, written to celebrate her reaching age 75, hence the title *Milepost 75,* reminds us that it is never too late to tackle what we may have thought were 'impossible dreams.' Ms. Richmond describes herself as a 'late bloomer,' so I recommend this book for anyone over 50 or 60 or 70 who hasn't had the chance yet to pursue some adventure travel and outdoor activities. She will show you what it takes!"

I enjoyed reading these early reviews! These readers had read my book and took the time to write thoughtful reviews. What a gift! I felt validated and inspired. Readers wrote that my book had made a difference in their lives. How they have started getting up and out again. That my trips helped them re-live some of their past travel experiences. That they had picked up old dreams that had been discarded or created new experiences they had never considered. That they were refusing to give up.

One woman emailed me saying she started pushing herself to tackle walking half marathons again after reading my book. "I had decided to stop and take those events off my list. I read your book and registered for one early next year." A gentleman said my book inspired him to hold onto the dream of hiking the Grand Canyon. Another woman burst into tears when she met me. "I was so disappointed that my injury prevented me from walking my usual fast pace that I just gave up and stopped walking. But you had to start over many times, and you never gave up. You gave me permission to start walking again, even if I never get back to my best pace. Thank you!" Then she hugged me. I get hugged a lot.

This review was from my friend, Jane, one of the women with whom I hiked the Camino. "Full disclosure that I am in this book and had read chapters while it was being written. I attribute my delay in reading the entire book to karma. I needed something to inspire me out of a 6-month funk, and this book was perfect. I laughed and cried and reminisced. I was in awe of how Sandi soldiered through serious physical issues and always came out smiling and full of gratitude. By the end of the book, I said, *Get over yourself and get out and walk!!* I think anyone who reads this book will find a message for themselves." Jane also sent me an email thanking me and suggesting we register for an upcoming walking event. She was determined to get "out of her funk" and back on track.

Jane's feedback warmed my heart and helped me discover a feedback theme I hadn't noticed earlier. For example, "Mrs. Richmond's memoirs of her passion for walking/hiking and perseverance through her medical conditions is inspiring. Last year I was told I'd eventually need a knee replacement, these stories have motivated me to get moving again and enjoy life. Her love of family and life was felt throughout the book." This reader read my book and felt encouraged to get moving even though she will have knee surgery. I started receiving similar feedback from readers who were afraid their active lives would be halted by hip or knee replacements. My surgery stories were resonating.

My other struggles also served as inspiration. One woman met me, hugged me, and started crying. "I had stopped walking completely because I was so discouraged by my slowing pace. I read *Milepost 75* and realized I could enjoy walking again even if I was slower. Thank you!"

And sometimes, my memoir provided a little nudge. I received this email after one of my book talks, "Thank you for being an inspiration and reminding me of the importance of being outside and enjoying the journey." Miriam, my American Lung Association stair-climbing buddy from Columbus texted, "I just finished *Milepost 75*, and it was a great read! So inspiring! You'll be happy to know I decided to add an extra loop on my walk at the Metropark yesterday to make it a 3-mile walk instead of 2, just because of your book."

Although most feedback came from aging readers, I even heard from others, much younger. This review, for example, "What an amazing story. She is a truly gifted and positive writer. Being in my late 40s I truly needed to hear the story. It's well written, very upbeat, and has inspired me to start my own journey." Another woman told me, "It's easy to see why seniors would appreciate reading your story, but it may be even more meaningful to people like me who are the same age you were when you finally got started on your active fitness path. It's not too late. The time to get going is now!" A young woman sent me a thank you note, writing, "Your book inspired me and has challenged me to walk, see, explore, and to travel."

So finally, the answer to your question, yes! My memoir helped create a new purpose for me, and it was the same one I discovered when I volunteered at the St Augustine Lighthouse. I could make a difference one person at a time. At St. Augustine, I could help people achieve their goal, their bucket list, their dream by climbing the lighthouse. And now, with *Milepost 75*, I can encourage readers to get started, stay moving forward, and never give up.

As I was working on the final edits to this book, I received a poignant message from Victoria, the daughter of one of my dear friends, Debbie, who was in the early stages of dementia. Debbie and I had been neighbors, friends, moms, raising our young daughters and toddler sons together, spending time walking and talking. We hiked Sabino. We shared milestone events. We had stayed connected through the years as our children grew up and we slowed down. Ours was a lifelong friendship.

Victoria wrote, "My mom has your book with her at all times. She loves reading passages throughout the day. She keeps it in her bag with her. I think of it as her safety book."

She even sent a picture of her mom, hunched over, her brow furrowed with concentration, studying my book with its worn pages. Perhaps somehow, my stories were helping her mom, my dear lifelong-friend recapture her own sweet memories.

My heart was broken. My heart was warmed. This was such precious feedback. It served as a profound reminder that my book could make a difference, one person at a time, in ways I never expected.

 HOW DID YOU MARKET YOUR BOOK?

Although I had hoped to sell lots of books, I didn't have a specific marketing strategy, just a gratitude strategy. Early on, my highest priority was to say thank you. I bought books in bulk so I could sign and send them to all those who had joined me on this journey.

It was quite the process. I eventually ended up signing and mailing almost 200 books to family, friends, every person who was included in the book, those who wrote blurbs, and all those who encouraged and supported me along the way.

I wrapped and mailed most books individually, becoming good friends with the clerk at the post office. She quickly learned the drill. "More media mail?" I nodded. She weighed, computed, stamped, and tossed into the bin. "Bye! See you tomorrow."

In one case I mailed 18 books in one box to Jonathan so he could deliver them to my neighbors and hand then out to women in our synagogue. Big help!

As soon as the books were delivered, the responses started bouncing back. "Thank you!" "I stayed up all night reading." "I read the first two chapters and was exhausted." "I opened the package, saw your book, and burst out crying. I know how much you wanted this. Thank you!"

Instead of a strategy, I simply scattered seeds of thanks. The seeds landed, planted, and germinated. Then, I started getting requests for book talks.

One friend, Ileine, read the copy I sent to her, then shared it with Monica, the resident lifestyle coordinator of Westminster St. Augustine retirement community who asked Ileine, "This would be a great book to share with our residents. Do you think Sandi would come here to give a book talk?"

Yes, I would. After the book talk, I had the opportunity to share hiking stories with several seniors, some in their 90s!

Arlene overheard Jonathan as he gave my book to Isabel at our synagogue. "Your mom is an author? I wonder if she would be willing to give a book talk at our Hadassah Summer Book Reviews program in July." Yes, I was. Yes, I did.

Jonathan helped me get set up and finagle the awkward microphone set up. Participants asked interesting questions about hiking, family trips, and how I wrote my book. They laughed at my jokes. I calmed my nerves that had been rattled and started enjoying myself. Grandsons, Flip and Sam, even attended. Flip took pictures. After the session, he gave me a solid thumbs up. When I asked Sam what he thought, he hesitated, then unlocked his eyes from his phone, gave me a big grin, and awarded me with a so-so horizontal thumb. He was fourteen. Good enough.

Synagogue Sisterhood members, Mindy, Ann, and Joyce scheduled a book talk for the following January. They were particularly interested in hearing about my job at Walt Disney World. Also, how I went back to school and studied harder after I did not score high enough when I took the GMAT the first time, impressed that I refused to give up. They even asked Jonathan and me about the hikes we were taking in the 7 Creeks Recreation Area. Shortly after the meeting, some participants emailed and asked if Jonathan and I would lead them on a group hike in a local preserve. What a great outcome. They came to my book talk; then wanted to take a walk.

My dear Page Turner book club scheduled *Milepost 75* for their September selection. Then three members, Pat, Peg, and Sally, took it a step further and created a book talk event for Grand Haven residents. Arnie and I had lived there for eight years. Many of our former neighbors showed up. Jonathan helped with greeting and welcoming the more than 50 attendees. During the Q&A session and after the meeting, I had the opportunity to hug old friends and answer more questions about writing my book.

My daughter-in-law, Lauren, arranged a lovely wine and dine meeting for me to share my memoir and spend a memorable evening with her good friends and fellow voracious readers.

And Isabel suggested I reach out to the owners of the Story & Song Bookstore Bistro/Center for Arts & Culture when she heard our family was planning to gather for the July 4th weekend on Fernandina Island. I contacted Mark and Donna. We had coffee while we chatted about our lives and my book. They also educated me on the importance of supporting independent bookstores.

And they hosted a Literary Luncheon (sold out!) for me and *Milepost 75*. Their publicity included the following:

> While we have many chapters in life, there are many new challenges in our story as we age. Sandra joins us with her book Milepost 75, part memoir, part travel guide, part best friend offering encouragement. Her book is a master class on aging!

Jonathan joined me, doing the heavy lifting as usual. He even created a slide presentation depicting my hiking adventures, a nice addition. Afterwards, as I signed books, we chatted about thriving after joint-replacement surgeries, hiking the Grand Canyon, and writing our memoirs. A few of us promised to stay in touch.

The recipients of the books I gifted continue to pass on their copies of *Milepost 75* to others. More people are reading my book. More book club meetings are on my schedule.

I'm certainly not a best-selling author, but I could be considered a best-sharing one.

My marketing recipe also included a dash of curiosity when I noticed taglines on several books—"prize-winning author of…" So, I decided to enter a few "contests," especially since they also offered editorial reviews as part of the package. I set my annual budget at $250 and so far, my investment has paid off.

I earned a "Gold Book" award from Literary Titan along with a lovely editorial review.

The $45 I invested to enter the Indie Author Reimagined Experience sponsored by the Tucson Festival of Books in Arizona (one of the premier book festivals in the country and even the world) produced significant returns. I had hoped to be selected for a panel, but that was a long shot, and was delighted to be awarded a selling, signing table for a three-hour slot in the Indie Author Pavilion. Thea, Steve, and Lynn helped me get set up. Thea stayed to support me the entire three hours. Lynn served as our official photographer. Steve helped me get my Square device connected to my new phone.

I checked in early and secured a super spot facing the walkway. People stopped by and perused my book. I gave them a bookmark, saying "no obligation." We exchanged smiles, and sometimes they bought a copy!

One woman walked up and hovered over the table with a copy of *Milepost 75* in her hand. "I read your book. You said if you inspired at least one person, you'd be satisfied. Well, I'm that person. You inspired me and I'd like you to sign my book."

Another woman lingered, holding the book, looking at the front, reading the back. She sighed. "I know I need this. I have a heart condition. My doctor and my husband tell me I need to start walking more, but I'm so scared," she said as she placed her hand over her heart. "It's $20? Let me see if I have the cash. I have $10. Let me go check with my husband."

I knew I didn't have to bargain, but she *needed* my book. I was afraid if she walked away, she might not return. "Take my book for $10. I believe it will help you."

She cocked her head, grinned, dug in her tiny pocketbook, and handed me the $10. I signed the book and gave it to her. She nodded, held it to her chest, thanked me, and walked away.

"Thea, I was worried about her. I believe my book can help her."

Thea smiled. "It's good to listen to your heart."

Time flew by. We chatted with the other authors in the tented pavilion, comfortably shaded from the Tucson sun, basking in the warmth of our own little community.

Festival participants continued to stroll by, some stopping, a few more buying.

The woman returned with *Milepost 75* pressed to her chest

and money in her hand. "Here's $20. Give me back my $10. My husband said you deserved full price for your book."

I accepted her $20; returned her $10.

We exchanged smiles and she walked away.

I took a big breath. My eyes burned. *Did not expect that.*

Thea murmured, "Good job."

I inadvertently created a marketing strategy consisting of gratitude, goodwill, free books, curiosity, caring community, and communication. It has paid off in ways I never imagined. Who knew?

HOW HAS YOUR LIFE CHANGED NOW THAT YOU ARE AN AUTHOR?

That heavy weight has vanished. I felt the same way when I finally completed the Grand Canyon rim-to-rim-to-rim 50/24. And when I completed my PhD.

Wanting to write a book had been nestled in my brain for 30 years, I couldn't wipe or rationalize it away. I knew if I didn't do it, it would stay there, reminding me that I *did not finish.* It is such a relief to say, "Finished!"

My life has expanded at an age when I fully expected it to shrink. My memories are more vivid because they're written in my memoir. I've met new people. Shared more stories. Heard more stories. Received more hugs.

And I continue to write. As I put the finishing touches on this book, responding to all the editing notes from Nathan, another son of Thea's, and my creative and capable editor for this book, I've started journaling ideas for a third memoir.

I embrace my expanded life that includes writing along with all my other priorities—family, friends, fitness, and community.

And I celebrate this amazing accomplishment, that I finally

wrote my book and got it published at the ripe old age of 80.

Conclusion

There were many unexpected delights associated with writing this manuscript. One big surprise was how much I had already learned about writing a book! Although I have maintained this is not a how-to book, perhaps some of the most valuable things I took away from this experience may help you.

So, as I begin to conclude my writing journey, here are some lessons I learned:

Ask for help even if it's risky, uncomfortable, and embarrassing. I would have never gotten unstuck if I hadn't reached out to Lynya. If you have any doubt, take the time to read the acknowledgements sections of a few of your favorite books and reflect on all the people most authors thank, frequently commenting, "I could not have done this without you."

Share your journey even if you're not completely sure you will reach your dream destination. When I finally built up the nerve to tell my Page Turners book club that I was writing a memoir, I immediately had a team of project managers, requesting and reviewing my progress each month.

Define your purpose at the beginning of your book and at the beginning of each chapter. And then adjust as you write and receive feedback. Read, reread, review, keep refining and defining.

As I look back, it helped me to break up my journey into sections. I secured the assistance I needed from Lynya. I wrote the first draft of my manuscript, long, clunky, and wordy, but without judgement to get it out of my head—usually. Then, I started editing. I stayed on track and did not get lost. I was able to stay in the present and not get blinded with worry about what the future would bring—most of the time.

Acknowledge and accept that some portions of your book will be cut. One of the first things I told Lynya was that I had learned from writing my dissertation that I could not fall in love with my words. Although it was hard to cut words and stories, it helped me to start with this expectation. Just remember they are never gone for good. Put them in a folder for future use. You won't be sorry. If you wrote them, keep them.

Embrace, appreciate, and accept caring and candid feedback—from your readers, family, coaches, publishers, and editors but balance this with trusting your gut. If an approach or story is important for you to keep, then keep it; however, be willing to flex if you receive feedback from multiple sources, especially those early readers.

Make writing a joyful facet of your life. Of course, there will be times you struggle and get stuck, but when you do, remember to dig deep, remember your purpose, and recapture your joy.

If you can, find a special someone to take this journey by your side. Someone to share the lows and celebrate the highs with you. Arnie was my soul mate, my partner, my cheerleader, my shoulder to lean on through the first half of my writing journey. He helped me from the beginning through the initial manuscript. Find yours—either in person or remote—someone who has your back and understands your heart.

Discover and rely on your team to serve as your coach, publisher, and editor. I was fortunate. I had the resources and good luck to work with Lynya, my writing coach. And my dear lifelong friend, Lynn, introduced me to Thea who then assigned Paul to serve as my editor.

Be patient. Be persistent. Slow down when you feel frantic. Speed up when you start to drag. Don't give up. Remember why you started this journey in the first place. Imagine what it will feel like when you cross the finish line. Keep writing. Celebrate step by step.

As I look back from the vantage point of my finish line, I can truly appreciate all the support I received from family, friends, and colleagues, and even people who didn't really know me. I expected some support because my family and friends are generally kind and thoughtful, but this was much more than I imagined.

Jonathan caught an incorrect reference in the front of my book to a blurb on the back cover. Rachel did a deep dive through the entire book. She made sure the names of events and locations were accurate. For example, I had called the Portland triathlon, "Tri for *the* Cure." She pointed out it was "Tri for *a* Cure." She also discovered I had written Rockland instead of Rockville, the town we stayed in before the One Day Hike.

I was overwhelmed by the generosity of other authors. First, the ones who took the time and effort to write blurbs for my book. In every case, they wrote lovely blurbs but also included thoughtful and inspiring messages to me—telling me my writing was good, my story compelling, and encouraging me to keep writing. During the past few months, I've met other authors. Each of them has volunteered to coach me, to share their ideas on marketing and promotion. In every case, when I thank them, their response has been, "We are colleagues, not competitors"

My readers made all the difference. Thank goodness I listened. They helped me understand what resonated with them in *Milepost 75* and then asked the questions that formed the basis of *Aging Adventurously at 80: How I Wrote a Book and Got it Published*.

This second book was begging to be written. I pitched the idea to Thea. She loved it. "It's a great way to answer all those questions your readers keep asking you. You can also share your own personal journey and all you have learned. You know how to describe the exciting things you have already accomplished. This is simply one more adventure story."

I was pleasantly surprised when I realized I could write this current book with greater ease. It felt natural to write another memoir about how I wrote my first memoir since I had learned so much from writing *Milepost 75*!

I didn't need a writing coach this time because I had already learned so much from Lynya. The format was easy. I simply started documenting the questions I had received and answered them. Then I started digging into questions of my own and answering those too. Writing this manuscript was fast and fun. I started in early July and finished with the first draft in late December.

I knew I would still need my publisher and editor for fine-tuning, formatting, and all the steps it takes to transform a manuscript into a book. And during these past few months, I've had the opportunity to work with Nathan as my editor, learning even more as I delved into this new and exciting adventure with a new book and new editor. What a delight.

Writing this book reinforced just how important, satisfying, and necessary it is for me to continue writing.

And so, another big surprise was that writing had become a part of my lifestyle, part of my life. Not just jotting notes, like in the journal I had written for myself since I was in my 30s, but also writing my next book—for myself and others. I had spent so many years on *Milepost 75* it was hard to stop. I already have stories typed and notes gathered for the next *Milepost* memoir.

And even now, as I finish this current memoir, I ask myself, *What would I do if I decided to stop writing?* Even though my life continues to be full, I think it might leave a gaping hole.

My biggest lesson since I first started writing *Milepost 75* way back in 2018 may be that walking helps my writing. It unlocks ideas, takes me to a higher level and deeper place in my head and heart where I discover lost memories and new ways of expressing my thoughts. I don't think I have ever returned from a walk without some new perspective or perception.

I'm delighted when readers tell me they are inspired to get out and walk after reading *Milepost 75*. I just read that spending a little time moving each day may even slash the risk of developing dementia by almost 30%. My daily moving choice is walking outside every day. Many days I walk 2-3 miles, some days longer, some days shorter, but I get outside and move for a few minutes every day. Walking calms me down. Walking makes me healthy and strong. Walking makes me a better writer.

Also, I thoroughly enjoy giving book talks. I did not expect that. But, when I think back to my career, especially my last two jobs at Walt Disney World and Limited Brands, I enjoyed facilitating learning and development sessions. I consider myself an introvert, but when I'm passionate about a topic and well prepared, then a little magic happens. The audience connects, they laugh, sometimes cry, ask questions, and even hug me when the session ends. Now the same thing is happening with my book talks. Another gift.

I still marvel at how much I learned about me and my life by writing and then reading my memoir. For example, it didn't dawn on me that I had a walking relationship with every member of my family. That our many walks and talks had created a special bond—perhaps even unique. Not something every family has.

As I read my book and received feedback from others, I realized even more how precious my relationship with Arnie was. How it grew stronger as we aged. As he grew weaker. We still had our ups and downs, but somehow, someway, we had ended up with a beautiful life story. All those choices. Decisions. Priorities. Steps taken. Talking. Listening. Understanding. Honesty. Compassion. Love.

Writing *Milepost 75* has helped keep Arnie alive in many unexpected ways. And that's the biggest and best gift of all.

When I consider all that has transpired, especially since *Milepost 75* was published, I think it happened for me at just the right time in my life, at just the right age.

Now I have more perspective, patience, and peace. Perhaps if this had materialized when I was younger, even 50 or 60, I may have been more frantic, driven to rush through the writing process, frustrated with the lag in sales, unable to see the big picture, my true purpose.

At 81, I spend much of my time giving thanks. My heart is warmed when someone tells me my book made a difference, gave them permission to get unstuck and start walking again, to walk on a new trail, to start writing their own book, to ask their children to take more trips together with them, to chase their dream, to keep moving forward, step by step.

Thank you for reading this book. I hope it answered your questions. I hope it was interesting and fun to read.

I hope my journey got you to the starting line.

I hope you take a chance on you.

I hope you capture that dream and write your own book.

I hope you start writing.

I hope you start now.

APPENDIX A
INITIAL FRAMEWORK EXAMPLE

Here is an example of my initial framework for what ultimately ended up being "Chapter 1: Milepost 45: Finding My Starting Line." I eventually dropped my original Chapter 1 and used the most interesting and compelling stories in my Introduction

CHAPTER 2: START, THEN TRY, TRY AGAIN

PURPOSE: One of the many dear readers who helped me with this book asked, "When did you start moving like this? How did you get started? For as long as I've known you, you've impressed me with your somewhat crazy passion for pushing yourself physically. Why are you so driven?"

STORY: I did not discover my fitness passion until I was 45, but once I did, I kept trying, never gave up, achieved my first big goal and transformed my life.

LESSON: It doesn't matter how late you start. What matters is finding something that touches your heart and soul. Once you find it, never, never let it go.

APPENDIX B
TITLE "BRAIN DUMP"

1. One More Year in My Adventure Land
2. One More Year: One Really Long Day
3. Let Me Get This straight: You're 75 & You Take This Hike?
4. Celebrating 75 and Taking a Hike
5. Turning 75 and Taking a Hike
6. Make Steps Count at 75
7. Counting Steps at 75 with Tribe, Trips, Trails
8. Celebrating 75 with Trails, Trips, & Tribe
9. Marking 75 - Making It Count
10. Help Me Get This Straight: You Turn 75 & Take This Hike?
11. Slow walking through 75: Tribe, Trips and Trails
12. Stepping through my 70s; Tribe, trips, and trails
13. Just One More Year of Big Slow Walks
14. Final Year Slow Walking on My Way to 75
15. Miles to Go Before I Cut Back
16. My Year of Slow Walking Through 75
17. You Turned 75 and This is How You Celebrate?
18. Why? At 75? Would You Walk that Far?
19. Slow Walking Through 75
20. Celebrating 75 with Trips, Trails, Trees, & Tribe
21. Slow Walking, Sharing Moments, Savoring Memories at 75
22. 75th year: Miles, Moments, & Memories
23. My 75th Year, My Way
24. My Way Through 75
25. Stepping Through 75
26. 75 and Stepping
27. Steps, Stairs, Tribe, Treks, and Trails Through 75
28. Celebrating 75 one step at a time
29. Oh Yes, I Can: I Have To
30. My Walks through 75

31. Being 75, Now or Never
32. My 75, Now or Never
33. Turning 75 All Year
34. Turning 75, Taking Next Steps
35. Making Moments All Through 75
36. Making My 75 Memories
37. My Step, Slow Step Through 75
38. Joyful Journey Through 75
39. Journey Through 75
40. Year-Long Journey Through 75
41. Year-Long Journey Through 75: It's Now or Never
42. It's Now or Never: Year-Long Journey Through 75
43. Turning 75: Making It Count
44. Celebrating 75: Making It Count
45. My 75 List and Life
26. 75 to 76 Journey
47. Getting Better at 75
48. Turning 75 with Nothing to Prove and Everything to Gain
49. Making the Best of 75
50. Finding New Joy at 75
51. Never Been 75 Before: Who Knew?
52. Trail from 75 to 76
53. Joy and Gratitude Along "My-Way 75"
54. Being 75, Endings, Beginnings, Going the Distance
55. Being 75, Growing the Distance with Gratitude and Joy
56. Trail Magic from 75 to 76
57. Walking Through My Wonder-Filled 75th Year
58. Walking for My Life at 75
59. Being 75, My List, My Way
60. Hiking 75 with Nature, Nurture, and Joy
61. Beautiful Walks Through 75
62. Stepping Along the Trail from 75 to 76
64. Walking Through 75, One Step at a Time
65. Making 75 Count

66. One More Year: Making the Most of Milestone 75
67. Hiking Through My Elder World of 75
68. Milestone 75: Life, List, Lessons, and Love
69. Making the Most of Milestone 75
70. Being 75 and Traveling Along the Seventies Trail
71. Hiking Through My Seventies, Celebrating 75
72. Celebrating 75: Going the Distance One Step at a Time
73. Slow Walking through My Seventies: Celebrating Milestone
74. Slow Walking through My 70s: Celebrating Mile Post 75
75. Walking Through My 70s: Exploring, Enjoying, Embracing
76. Who Knew Slow Walking Through 70s Could Be So Much fun?
77. The Joy of Climbing, Hiking, Traveling, Walking Through My 70s
78. The Joy of Walking Slowly Through My 70s & Celebrating
79. Turning 75; Taking Some Hikes
80. At 75, It's Now or Never
81. Being 75, Doing It Now or Never
82. Turning 75, Getting It Done Before 76
83. Midpoint in Your 70s, Making It Count
84. Getting It Done at 75
85. Hiking Those Trails From 75 to 76
86. Being 75: Now or Never
87. I'm at 75 and Will Never Pass This Way Again
88. I've Never Been 75 Before!
89. Making the Most of 75
90. My "Now or Never" Year of 75
91. More Walking Adventures After 75?
92. My 75 – "Now or Never" Celebration
93. Oh Yes, I Can! Slow Walking Through 75
94. One More Year of Long Walks at 75
95. Making the Most of Mile Post 75
96. The Joy of Walking at 75
97. Trail and Tribe Walking at 75

98. Late Start at 45; Long Walk at 75
99. 75 Trail; List, Lessons, Love, and Life
100. Going My Distance at 75
101. Going My Distance My Way at 75
102. New Trail at 45; Looping Back at 75
103. Late Start at 45: Long Trek at 75
104. My Path from 45 to 75
105. My Path Taken from 45 to 75
106. Trailhead 45: Milepost 75
107. Finding My Passion at 45: Persisting, Moving Forward at 75
108. Passion 45: Persistence 75
109. Path Taken at 45: Continuing the Journey at 75
110. Path Discovered at 45: Moving Onward at 75

APPENDIX C
UNSENT QUERY LETTER
TO PUBLISHER

Dear Thea,

I have read your book along with several other books published by Flint Hills Publishing and have also learned more about you and your approach by following your Facebook group and seeing firsthand some of the many ways you educate, engage, and support emerging authors. And so, after receiving several gentle nudges from my dear friend Lynn Murphy I'm submitting my 100-word bio, Table of Contents, and Introduction to my memoir, *Milepost 75: An Ode to the Miles, Moments, and Memories of My 75th Year* in the hope that you will accept my book for publication.

In my research I found many books that told tales of active seniors who are natural-born athletes, elite, first-place, gold-medal seniors who are fast enough, strong enough, tough enough to qualify for most competitive events. I've read about many seniors who have hiked entire trails like the AT or PCT, who are the oldest to hike high or to finish an Ironman, and those who started slow, yet managed to come up from behind and pass all the others, get to the front, rise to the top, receive the awards and accolades. But I could not find any memoirs about the rest of us seniors who would never achieve those heights or level of mastery.

My memoir is about staying actively, happily fit after getting a late start and usually ending up somewhere in the back of the pack. It's the story of someone who is not the best, fastest, or strongest. I am a solid member of the generation that is living longer, but in some cases, not necessarily stronger. This is a good time for people to read my story especially in light of what we learned about health and longevity during COVID. Many of those who survived, even thrived were the ones who stayed happily, actively fit.

I've learned that it's never too late to start. Also, that most of us have easy access to paths, sidewalks, even roads where we can move forward and breathe deep, outside, in the sun even the rain or snow.

This book tells the story of how I got a late start on my path of an active lifestyle. It also provides an opportunity for armchair travelers to share in some of my adventures both here and abroad, all taken after I turned 70. I explain how my retirement became a beginning, not an end. This is not a how-to book but more a tale of trips I've taken, trails I've hiked, lessons I've learned. It's a story about flexibility of body and soul, of compromise, compassion, and community. A story of family, friends, fellow hikers, and volunteers.

I think this is the right time for this book. It's unique because of everything it is not. Not about winning, qualifying, or being the best. It's simply a book about a few things that have worked for me, that have helped me be the best I can be and maybe help others do the same. It's a good time to be so inspired by an active achievable lifestyle that we embrace it with gusto as if our lives depended on it, so we can keep going strong into our 80s and beyond.

Warmly,
Sandi Richmond

APPENDIX D
Bookmark (printed in full color)

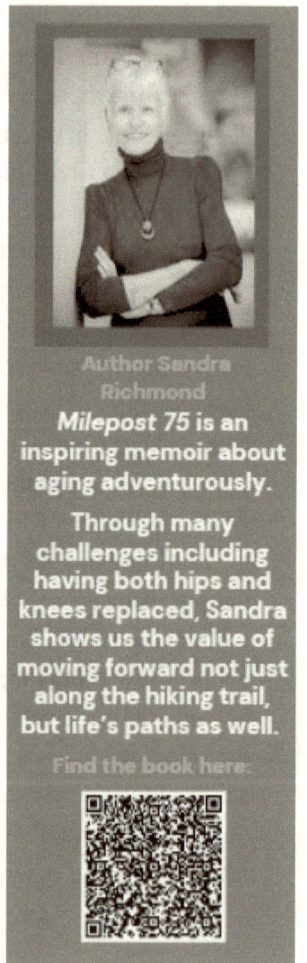

APPENDIX E
INSERT PLACED IN GIFTED BOOKS
(Printed in color: 4 per 8.5 by 11 sheet)

Thank you for your support of *Milepost 75!*

While it takes time and effort to write a book, MARKETING that book takes a ton of GRIT! Your support in helping Sandi get the word out is much appreciated! You can help by:

- Leaving an honest review on Amazon;
- Recommending the book to your friends;
- Invite Sandi to your book club or other events. She can "Zoom-in" or perhaps even visit in person!

Here's to "Aging Adventurously" & to creating a well-read world!

Thea Rademacher, JD
Publisher

Flint Hills Publishing

ACKNOWLEDGMENTS

Thank you!

To my readers. For reading *Milepost 75*, for your feedback, and especially for all your questions about how I managed to write my first book and get it published at 80. While my first memoir was embedded in my head for almost 30 years before I started writing, the seeds for this second book were planted and started germinating in around four weeks. As soon as I heard all your questions about how I managed to get *Milepost 75* written and published, I started to wonder, *What if I write another book that answers all those questions?* If you had not asked those questions, I would have never considered answering them in another memoir. You and your curiosity made this happen. I listened to you—and wrote this book.

To my stalwart Page Turners book club who joined me on my journey, asking questions and offering support. Through the years, members came and went, but the ones who cheered me on and learned with me from the beginning were Dianne Robichaud, Dale Curran, Paula Iuliucci, Marian Penzo, Andrea Latish, and the late and beloved Sandy Lee. A special hug of gratitude to Peg Pettingell, Sally Castellari, and Pat Malak for all the time, effort, care, kindness, and compassion they invested in their sponsorship of the Grand Haven Community book talk.

To my Jacksonville sisterhood: Ann Stone, Isabel Balotin, Mindy Grinnan, Susan Board, Jackie Simms, Miriam Greenhut, Sheila Slavkin, Robyn Kay, Rhoda London, Marcia Luettchau, Cathy Winterfield, Ruth Nachman, Karen Backilman, Joyce Elkin, Marie Reitzes, Jill Metlin, Goldie Lansky, Randee Steinberg, Barbara Teitelman, Linda Weinstein, Elaine Hodz, Nikki Levinson-Lustgarten, Joan Waitz, Eve Aptheker, Susan Nadler,

Phyllis Fischer, Helen Hill, Arlene Fonda Korr, Felice Caliestro, the Hadassah Book Group. The list keeps growing. Thank you for your support and encouragement!

To my friends, extended family, EverWalk partners, fellow authors, FHP team, and neighbors: Cheryl and Tim Stippler, June Hershey, Karen Kane McDonnell, Maryellen Cortese, Mindy Oksenhorn, Cheryle Easton, Barbara Bush, Melissa Bowersock, Tom Zoellner, Sharon Leino, Royce Fitts, Clyde Toland, Greg German, Suzanne Day, Nancy Powers, Linda and Larry Morabito, Ellen and John Bertolacci, Mark and Marcia Thornally, Michele Orlowski, Michelle Mansell, Elise Mansell, Anita Olson, Saza, Kewang, Robin Sturm, Daryl Magaw-Michaels, Madalyn Benjamin, Lisa Harrington, Christine and David Gallagher, Kathie Gargiulo, Monica Hicks, Ileine Hoffman, Gina and Dave Johnson, Mary Cooper, Cathy Kasriel, Jane Altenhofen, Joan Klopf, Sandy Hall, Donna Larsen, Sandy West, Wil Hessert, Art and Louise Dyke, Christy Reves, Jade Mortimer, Ann Marie Rakovic, Joan Tierney, Linda Napier Prescott, Nancy Hanauer, Barbara Waterman Peters, David Archer, Carrie Traylor, Cindy Maxwell, Laura Peterson, Linda Hurst, Tanya O'Brien, Cathy Fulton, Ronnie Botnick, Susanne Galler, Mel Grosvenor, Barbara Wells, Rachel Waldorf, Carole Sheehan, Deb Tinajero, Victoria Bray, Suzanne and Kenny Cummins, Nancy Peddle, Fuzzy Adelman, Laurel Zulliger, and the Loosie Goosey Sisterhood book club. This list, too, keeps growing.

To Story and Song Bistro owners, Mark Kauffman and Donna Paz Kauffman who shared their life stories with me and listened to mine. You educated and embraced me and opened a whole new world of independent bookstores for me.

To Lynya Floyd who got me started on my writing journey with *Milepost 75* and continued to encourage me as I wrote this second memoir.

To Lynn Murphy my lifelong friend with her sturdy shoulder to lean on, guiding me on every step of my writing and publishing journey, and joining me as the perfect learning partner on our annual Tucson Festival of Books adventures.

To the Flint Hills Publishing Team: Steve Fredrickson for his financial navigating and nurturing support, Paul for helping me dig deep, write better, and heal as he edited *Milepost 75*, Nathan for his exquisite and insightful editing, giving this book the additional depth and heart that was missing in my initial manuscript. And Thea, my publisher who made this all come to fruition and along the way became my muse, my teacher, my friend, my soulmate.

To my dear family: In-laws, Rob Litz and Lauren Cortese; grandsons, Jonathan Litz, Andrew Litz, Jonathan Richmond, and Samuel Richmond.

To my favorite daughter: Rachel Elaine Litz. To my favorite son: Jonathan Robert Richmond. You offer your hands to keep me steady and your shoulders for balance. You make me laugh at myself when I worry, offer perspective when I catastrophize, and provide solace when I cry. You fill my life with love. Because of you, I am whole.

And to Arnie. The memories of our happy years together sustain me. I miss you. I love you.

ABOUT THE AUTHOR

Sandra Richmond, PhD, did not fully embrace her active lifestyle until her mid-40s. Despite having arthritis, atrial fibrillation, spinal fusion surgery, and joint replacement surgeries in both hips and knees, she has slow-walked several marathons, half marathons, 50, 15, 10, and 5Ks, supporting worthy causes and happily encouraging others to join her in these walker-friendly events. She has completed events with every member of her family, creating unique and precious memories. An avid hiker, she has taken on the Grand Canyon over 30 times. After 70, Sandra incorporated adventure travel into her post-retirement life and has taken on challenging treks including the Inca Trail in Peru, the Camino de Santiago in Spain, Hadrian's Wall Path in England, and the West Highland Way in Scotland. She divides her time between Maryland and Florida.

www.milepoststories.com

Follow Sandra on Facebook: Milepost Stories

www.ingramcontent.com/pod-product-compliance
Lightning Source LLC
Chambersburg PA
CBHW031429120626
46545CB00006B/2324